Self-Help for Narcissism

Crafted by Skriuwer

Copyright © 2024 by Skriuwer.

All rights reserved. No part of this book may be used or reproduced in any form whatsoever without written permission except in the case of brief quotations in critical articles or reviews.

For more information, contact : **kontakt@skriuwer.com** (www.skriuwer.com)

Table of Contents

1. Understanding Narcissism
1.1 What is Narcissism?
1.2 Types of Narcissism: Overt, Covert, and More
1.3 The Root Causes of Narcissistic Behavior
1.4 The Narcissism Spectrum: Healthy vs. Unhealthy Narcissism
1.5 Narcissism in Today's Society: How Culture Shapes Self-Centeredness

2. Recognizing Narcissism in Yourself
2.1 Signs You May Be Struggling with Narcissism
2.2 Common Patterns of Narcissistic Thoughts and Behaviors
2.3 The Impact of Narcissism on Relationships
2.4 Self-Reflection and Accountability: Beginning Your Healing Journey
2.5 Recognizing Defensiveness: How to Overcome Denial

3. Narcissism and Relationships
3.1 The Role of Narcissism in Personal Relationships
3.2 How Narcissism Can Lead to Toxic Patterns
3.3 Learning to Recognize Empathy Deficits in Yourself
3.4 Building Healthy Boundaries in Relationships
3.5 Repairing Relationships Damaged by Narcissistic Behavior

4. The Narcissism-Empathy Disconnect
4.1 Understanding Empathy: Cognitive vs. Emotional Empathy
4.2 Why Narcissism Blocks True Empathy
4.3 Reconnecting with Empathy: Techniques for Developing Compassion
4.4 Practicing Active Listening and Perspective-Taking
4.5 How Cultivating Empathy Strengthens Relationships

5. Breaking the Cycle of Narcissistic Behavior
5.1 Identifying the Core Fears Behind Narcissism
5.2 Shifting from External Validation to Internal Validation
5.3 Practicing Humility: Learning to Accept Imperfection
5.4 Developing Gratitude: A Key to Healing Narcissistic Tendencies
5.5 Building Healthy Self-Esteem Without Narcissism

6. Healing from Narcissistic Traits
6.1 Acknowledging the Need for Change
6.2 The Importance of Vulnerability in Growth
6.3 Learning to Apologize and Repair
6.4 Forgiving Yourself: Letting Go of Past Mistakes
6.5 Rebuilding Trust in Relationships

7. Coping with Narcissistic Injuries
7.1 Understanding Narcissistic Injuries: Emotional Wounds that Trigger Narcissistic Responses
7.2 Identifying Triggers and Learning to Respond Differently
7.3 Managing Criticism and Rejection: Tools for Handling Ego Bruises
7.4 Building Emotional Resilience and Coping Skills
7.5 Moving from Reactivity to Emotional Stability

8. Self-Awareness: The Key to Transformation
8.1 The Role of Mindfulness in Self-Awareness
8.2 Practicing Self-Reflection: Journaling and Other Techniques
8.3 Developing Emotional Intelligence to Understand Your Feelings and Reactions
8.4 Embracing Feedback and Constructive Criticism
8.5 Tracking Personal Growth: Measuring Progress Over Time

9. Transforming Narcissistic Habits
9.1 Shifting from Self-Centeredness to Serving Others
9.2 Creating a Daily Practice of Gratitude and Generosity
9.3 Learning to Accept Criticism and Grow from It
9.4 Moving from Self-Promotion to Humility
9.5 Sustaining Long-Term Change

10. Healthy Boundaries: Learning to Respect Others
10.1 Understanding the Importance of Boundaries in Relationships
10.2 Setting Personal Boundaries Without Guilt
10.3 Recognizing and Respecting the Boundaries of Others
10.4 Dealing with Boundary Violations in a Healthy Way
10.5 Balancing Self-Care and Responsibility in Relationships

11. Narcissism in the Workplace
11.1 How Narcissism Manifests in Professional Settings
11.2 Managing Power and Authority Without Narcissism
11.3 Collaborative Work vs. Self-Centered Leadership
11.4 How Narcissism Affects Team Dynamics
11.5 Cultivating Empathy and Respect in Professional Relationships

12. Dealing with Narcissism in Others
12.1 Recognizing Narcissistic Traits in Others
12.2 Setting Boundaries with Narcissistic People
12.3 Navigating Conflict with Narcissistic Individuals
12.4 Protecting Your Self-Esteem and Well-Being
12.5 When to Walk Away from Narcissistic Relationships

13. Self-Compassion vs. Narcissism
13.1 The Difference Between Healthy Self-Love and Narcissism
13.2 Practicing Self-Compassion While Avoiding Narcissism
13.3 The Role of Self-Forgiveness in Personal Growth
13.4 How to Cultivate Self-Worth Without Seeking External Validation
13.5 Developing a Growth Mindset

14. Mindfulness and Narcissism
14.1 How Mindfulness Can Help Curb Narcissistic Behaviors
14.2 Daily Practices to Cultivate Awareness and Presence
14.3 Using Meditation to Manage Ego and Narcissistic Tendencies
14.4 The Role of Gratitude in Shifting Focus Away from Self-Centeredness
14.5 Developing a Practice of Letting Go: Releasing Control and Expectations

15. Narcissism in the Age of Social Media
15.1 How Social Media Reinforces Narcissism
15.2 The Constant Need for Validation Online
15.3 Balancing Self-Promotion with Authenticity
15.4 Developing a Healthy Relationship with Social Media
15.5 Unplugging: How to Disconnect for Mental Health

16. Emotional Healing and Growth
16.1 The Emotional Toll of Narcissism: Shame, Guilt, and Anger
16.2 Learning to Process Difficult Emotions
16.3 Releasing Negative Patterns and Creating New Emotional Habits
16.4 How Self-Compassion Leads to Emotional Growth
16.5 Finding Inner Peace: Long-Term Emotional Health Strategies

17. Rebuilding Your Life After Narcissism
17.1 The Importance of Accountability in Personal Growth
17.2 Taking Responsibility for Past Mistakes
17.3 How to Set and Achieve Personal Goals Without Narcissism
17.4 Rebuilding Relationships with Integrity and Respect
17.5 Living a More Authentic, Empathetic Life

18. The Role of Therapy in Healing Narcissism
18.1 Finding the Right Therapist for Narcissistic Traits
18.2 The Benefits of Cognitive Behavioral Therapy for Narcissism
18.3 How Group Therapy Can Help Build Empathy and Connection
18.4 Self-Help Books and Resources for Narcissism Recovery
18.5 The Long-Term Commitment to Healing and Growth

19. Success Without Narcissism
19.1 Redefining Success in Your Life: Moving Away from External Validation
19.2 Developing a Healthy Work-Life Balance
19.3 Finding Fulfillment in Helping Others
19.4 Practicing Gratitude and Humility in Achievements
19.5 Living a Life of Service and Contribution

20. Living a Fulfilling, Narcissism-Free Life
20.1 The Daily Practices for a Balanced, Narcissism-Free Life
20.2 Staying Grounded in Relationships: Emotional Awareness and Empathy
20.3 How to Build Long-Lasting, Authentic Connections with Others
20.4 Regular Self-Reflection: Staying Accountable to Personal Growth
20.5 Celebrating Personal Growth and Looking Ahead

Chapter 1

Understanding Narcissism

What is Narcissism?

Narcissism is a complex psychological construct that encompasses a range of behaviors, attitudes, and personality traits characterized by an excessive focus on oneself and a profound need for admiration. At its core, narcissism can be understood through the lens of self-centeredness and a lack of empathy for others, often manifesting as an inflated sense of self-importance and entitlement. While many individuals may exhibit narcissistic traits to some degree, it becomes a clinical concern when these traits become pervasive and detrimental to interpersonal relationships and overall functioning.

The term "narcissism" originates from the Greek myth of Narcissus, a youth who fell in love with his own reflection in a pool of water, ultimately leading to his demise. This myth encapsulates the essence of narcissism: a fixation on self-image and an inability to connect meaningfully with the external world. Within psychological literature, narcissism is often categorized into two distinct types: grandiose narcissism and vulnerable (or covert) narcissism. Grandiose narcissists typically exhibit overt self-confidence, assertiveness, and a need for admiration, while vulnerable narcissists may present as sensitive, insecure, and self-deprecating, yet still harbor deep-seated feelings of entitlement and self-importance.

Key Traits of Narcissism

1. Grandiosity: Individuals with narcissistic traits often possess an exaggerated sense of their own importance and achievements. They may believe they are special or unique, and they often expect recognition and admiration that is disproportionate to their accomplishments.

2. Need for Admiration: A hallmark of narcissism is the incessant need for validation and admiration from others. This craving can lead to manipulative behaviors aimed at garnering attention, often resulting in superficial relationships that lack depth and authenticity.

3. Lack of Empathy: One of the most defining traits of narcissism is a pronounced lack of empathy. Narcissistic individuals often struggle to recognize or value the feelings and needs of others, leading to exploitative or dismissive behaviors. This deficit in empathy can contribute to strained interpersonal relationships and conflicts.

4. Entitlement: Narcissists typically exhibit a sense of entitlement, believing that they deserve special treatment or recognition. This belief can manifest in frustration or anger when they perceive that their needs are not being met or when they face criticism.

5. Exploitation of Others: Narcissistic individuals may use others to achieve their own ends, viewing relationships primarily through a utilitarian lens. This exploitation can result in a pattern of inconsiderate or manipulative behavior, often leaving others feeling used or undervalued.

6. Envy and Jealousy: Many narcissists experience envy towards others who have what they desire, whether it be success, status, or relationships. This envy can drive a need to belittle or undermine others, reinforcing their own self-image.

7. Reactive Defensiveness: When confronted with criticism or perceived slights, individuals with narcissistic traits often react defensively. They may respond with anger, denial, or blame to protect their fragile self-esteem, further complicating their relationships.

8. Self-Absorption: Narcissism is characterized by a preoccupation with one's own interests, problems, and achievements, often leading to a myopic view of the world. This self-absorption can create a barrier to genuine connection and understanding with others.

Understanding narcissism requires a nuanced approach, recognizing that while certain traits may be present in many individuals, the impact of these traits can vary significantly. In clinical contexts, narcissistic traits can be assessed through established diagnostic criteria, such as those proposed in the Diagnostic and Statistical Manual of Mental Disorders (DSM-5), which outlines Narcissistic Personality Disorder (NPD) as a pervasive pattern of grandiosity, need for admiration, and a lack of empathy.

Ultimately, an awareness of narcissism and its traits can foster greater empathy and understanding for those affected, while also encouraging individuals to engage in self-reflection and personal growth. This understanding is crucial for navigating the complexities of relationships where narcissistic traits may be present, whether in oneself or in others.

Types of Narcissism: Overt, Covert, and More

Narcissism is a complex personality trait that manifests in various forms, each with distinct characteristics and underlying motivations. Understanding the different types of narcissism can help individuals recognize and address these traits within themselves and others. The primary classifications of narcissism include overt narcissism, covert narcissism, and other subtypes, each playing a unique role in interpersonal dynamics and self-perception.

Overt Narcissism

Overt narcissism, often referred to as grandiose narcissism, is characterized by an outward display of self-importance and superiority. Individuals exhibiting overt narcissism tend to be openly arrogant, boastful, and attention-seeking. They thrive on admiration and validation from others, often exaggerating their achievements and talents. This type of narcissist typically believes they are exceptional and may feel entitled to special treatment.

Overt narcissists are often easily recognizable due to their bold behaviors and assertive communication style. They may dominate conversations, disregard others' opinions, and manipulate situations to maintain the spotlight. While their confident exterior may appear attractive, it often masks deep-seated insecurities and a fragile self-esteem that relies heavily on external validation.

Covert Narcissism

In contrast, covert narcissism presents in a more subtle and less recognizable manner. Covert narcissists may not display overt arrogance or boastful behavior; instead, they often portray themselves as sensitive, introspective, or self-deprecating. However, this façade often conceals a deep-seated sense of entitlement and a preoccupation with their own needs and feelings.

Covert narcissists tend to feel victimized and may engage in passive-aggressive behaviors. They often seek validation through martyrdom or self-sacrifice, expecting others to recognize their sacrifices without openly asking for it. This type of narcissism can lead to a cycle of manipulation where the covert narcissist uses guilt or pity to elicit sympathy and admiration from others, while remaining largely unaware of their own narcissistic traits.

Other Subtypes of Narcissism

In addition to overt and covert narcissism, there are other subtypes that are worth noting:

1. Malignant Narcissism: This is a severe form of narcissism that includes traits of antisocial personality disorder. Malignant narcissists are manipulative, exploitative, and may engage in harmful behaviors towards others without remorse. They are driven by a desire for power and control, often leading to toxic relationships.

2. Communal Narcissism: Communal narcissists derive their self-worth from their perceived altruism and concern for others. They often present themselves as exceptionally caring and socially responsible, but their actions are frequently self-serving. They seek acknowledgment for their good deeds and may become resentful if they feel unappreciated.

3. Somatic Narcissism: Individuals with somatic narcissism are overly focused on their physical appearance and bodily health. They may obsess over fitness, beauty, and sexual appeal, often seeking admiration for their looks or lifestyle. This type of narcissist may use their physicality as a means to gain attention and validation.

4. Cerebral Narcissism: Cerebral narcissists derive their self-worth from their intellect and knowledge. They often flaunt their intelligence and expect others to recognize their superiority in this area. While they may not be as overtly attention-seeking as their somatic counterparts, they can still be dismissive of those they perceive as less knowledgeable.

Conclusion

Understanding the various types of narcissism, from overt to covert and beyond, highlights the diverse ways these traits can manifest in behavior and interpersonal relationships. Recognizing these patterns is essential for self-awareness and personal growth. By identifying which type resonates with one's own behaviors or those of others, individuals can begin to navigate the complexities of narcissism, fostering healthier relationships and promoting emotional well-being. Each type carries its own challenges, but with self-reflection and effort, individuals can work towards overcoming the debilitating aspects associated with narcissism.

The Root Causes of Narcissistic Behavior

Narcissism, characterized by an inflated sense of self-importance, a deep need for admiration, and a lack of empathy, often finds its roots in early childhood experiences and the broader context of personality development. Understanding these foundational elements is crucial for individuals seeking to comprehend their own behaviors or those of others who exhibit narcissistic traits.

Childhood Experiences

The early years of life are formative, shaping an individual's personality, self-esteem, and interpersonal dynamics. Several childhood experiences can significantly contribute to the development of narcissistic traits:

1. Overvaluation by Parents: Children who are excessively praised or overvalued by their parents may develop a grandiose self-image. This can manifest as an expectation of admiration from others, leading to narcissistic behaviors in adulthood. Such overvaluation might stem from parents projecting their unfulfilled ambitions or desires onto their children, inadvertently placing undue pressure to succeed and maintain a façade of perfection.

2. Emotional Neglect: Conversely, children who experience emotional neglect may develop narcissistic traits as a defense mechanism. When parents fail to provide emotional support or validation, children may internalize feelings of inadequacy. To compensate, they might adopt narcissistic behaviors as a way of seeking the attention and validation they lacked. This often creates a cycle where the individual feels they must constantly prove their worth to themselves and others.

3. Trauma and Abuse: Experiences of trauma, including physical, emotional, or sexual abuse, can lead some individuals to develop narcissistic traits as a coping strategy. The defense of grandiosity can shield them from the pain and shame associated with their traumatic experiences, allowing them to maintain a sense of control and superiority over their emotions and circumstances.

4. Parental Role Modeling: Children often learn behaviors by observing their parents. If a child grows up in an environment where narcissistic behaviors are modeled—whether through a parent's entitlement, lack of empathy, or need for control—they may adopt similar patterns in their own behavior. This learned behavior can be reinforced by the child's interactions with their peers and broader social environment.

Personality Development

Beyond childhood experiences, personality development plays a crucial role in the formation of narcissistic traits. Several psychological theories provide insight into how personality may develop in a way that fosters narcissism:

1. Self-Concept Formation: The development of a self-concept is a vital aspect of personality development. Individuals with narcissistic tendencies may have an unstable or distorted self-concept, shaped by early interactions and feedback from caregivers. This instability can lead to a reliance on external validation to maintain a sense of self-worth, resulting in narcissistic behaviors as a way to reinforce their self-image.

2. Attachment Styles: Psychological theories of attachment suggest that early relationships with caregivers can influence personality. Children who develop insecure attachment styles—characterized by anxiety, avoidance, or ambivalence—may resort to narcissistic behaviors as a means of navigating their relationships. For example, an anxious attachment style might lead to possessiveness and a need for admiration, while an avoidant style could foster a lack of empathy and a focus on self-preservation.

3. Coping Mechanisms: As individuals navigate the complexities of life, those with narcissistic traits often employ maladaptive coping mechanisms. Instead of confronting vulnerabilities or insecurities, they may inflate their self-worth and diminish the importance of others' feelings. This coping strategy can create a cycle of self-centeredness that becomes increasingly ingrained in their personality.

In conclusion, the root causes of narcissistic behavior are deeply intertwined with childhood experiences and personality development. By understanding these factors, individuals can begin to unravel the complexities of their own behaviors or those around them, paving the way for self-reflection, healing, and growth. Recognizing the significance of early experiences and personality dynamics is essential for fostering healthier relationships and mitigating narcissistic tendencies in adulthood.

The Narcissism Spectrum: Healthy vs. Unhealthy Narcissism

Narcissism is often perceived solely as a negative trait, associated with self-centered behavior, lack of empathy, and a need for excessive admiration. However, understanding narcissism as a spectrum can provide a more nuanced view, distinguishing between healthy and unhealthy manifestations of narcissistic traits.

Healthy Narcissism

Healthy narcissism refers to a balanced sense of self-worth and self-esteem. Individuals exhibiting healthy narcissism possess a positive self-image and confidence that empowers them to pursue their goals and ambitions without undermining others. They recognize their own strengths and achievements while also respecting the value and contributions of those around them.

Key characteristics of healthy narcissism include:

1. Self-Confidence: Individuals with healthy narcissism exhibit a strong sense of self-belief. They are able to pursue their goals with determination, which can inspire others and lead to positive outcomes in both personal and professional settings.

2. Resilience: Healthy narcissists tend to bounce back from setbacks effectively. They can accept constructive criticism and view failures as opportunities for growth, which fosters both personal and relational development.

3. Empathy: Unlike their unhealthy counterparts, those with healthy narcissistic traits can empathize with others. They recognize the emotions and needs of those around them, allowing them to form meaningful connections and relationships.

4. Boundary Respect: Healthy narcissists understand the importance of personal boundaries and respect the boundaries of others. They are confident enough to express their needs while also valuing the needs of others.

5. Self-Care: Individuals in this category prioritize self-care and self-improvement, leading to a fulfilling life that balances personal aspirations with social responsibility.

Unhealthy Narcissism
On the opposite end of the spectrum lies unhealthy narcissism, which is characterized by an inflated sense of self-importance and a pervasive need for validation from others. This form of narcissism can lead to toxic behaviors and detrimental effects on relationships.

Key characteristics of unhealthy narcissism include:

1. Entitlement: Unhealthy narcissists often believe they deserve special treatment and recognition without having to earn it. This sense of entitlement can lead to frustration and anger when their expectations are not met.

2. Lack of Empathy: A hallmark of unhealthy narcissism is the inability to empathize with others. These individuals may struggle to recognize or care about the feelings and needs of those around them, leading to conflicts and relational strain.

3. Excessive Need for Admiration: Unhealthy narcissists require constant validation from others to maintain their self-esteem. This need can manifest as attention-seeking behavior and may result in superficial relationships based on admiration rather than genuine connection.

4. Defensiveness and Reactivity: When faced with criticism or perceived slights, unhealthy narcissists often react defensively or aggressively. This inability to accept feedback can hinder personal growth and damage relationships.

5. Manipulative Behavior: Individuals with unhealthy narcissistic traits may resort to manipulation to achieve their goals or maintain their self-image. This behavior can create an environment of distrust and emotional harm for those around them.

Finding Balance on the Spectrum
Understanding the spectrum of narcissism is crucial for personal growth and relationship

health. Healthy narcissism fosters self-confidence and resilience, enabling individuals to thrive while nurturing their connections with others. In contrast, unhealthy narcissism can lead to isolation, conflict, and emotional turmoil.

To navigate this spectrum, self-awareness is key. Individuals should reflect on their behaviors and motivations, seeking to cultivate healthy narcissistic traits while addressing and mitigating unhealthy ones. Engaging in practices such as mindfulness, empathy development, and building emotional intelligence can facilitate this process, allowing for a more balanced, fulfilling life where one can appreciate their worth without diminishing others.

Recognizing where one falls on this spectrum is the first step toward fostering healthier relationships and a more authentic self. By embracing the positive aspects of narcissism while addressing the harmful traits, individuals can embark on a journey of growth and transformation.

Narcissism in Today's Society: How Culture Shapes Self-Centeredness

In contemporary society, narcissism appears to be a pervasive issue, with self-centeredness increasingly normalized and even celebrated. This phenomenon can be traced to several cultural factors, including the rise of social media, consumerism, and the shifting values surrounding success and identity. Understanding how these elements interact with and shape narcissistic traits is crucial for addressing the consequences they have on relationships and individual well-being.

The Influence of Social Media

One of the most significant cultural influences contributing to narcissistic behaviors is the advent of social media. Platforms like Instagram, Facebook, and TikTok provide users with a stage to showcase their lives, often curating an idealized version of reality. This constant exposure to the "highlights" of others' lives fosters a culture of comparison, leading individuals to seek validation through likes, comments, and shares. The pursuit of online approval can cultivate a sense of self-worth that is contingent on external feedback, reinforcing narcissistic tendencies. Many users may develop a heightened need for admiration, leading to a cycle where self-esteem is tied to social media engagement rather than intrinsic qualities or accomplishments.

Moreover, the anonymity and distance provided by online platforms can diminish empathetic responses. People may feel emboldened to express self-centered views or engage in negative behaviors, such as cyberbullying, without the immediate repercussions that face-to-face interactions would entail. This disconnect can further entrench narcissistic behavior, as individuals become desensitized to the feelings and needs of others.

Consumerism and Materialism
Consumer culture also plays a pivotal role in shaping narcissistic tendencies. The marketing industry often promotes a message of individualism, suggesting that personal worth is tied to possessions and status. Advertisements that emphasize luxury, beauty, and success can perpetuate the belief that self-value is derived from external markers. As a result, individuals may prioritize material gain and self-promotion over collective well-being or community engagement, fostering a self-centered mindset.

This focus on materialism can also lead to competition among peers, as people strive to outdo one another in terms of possessions, experiences, and social status. Such competition can create an environment where empathy and altruism are sidelined, as individuals concentrate on their own advancement rather than nurturing relationships or contributing to the greater good.

Shifting Values and Identity
Cultural narratives surrounding success and identity have shifted significantly in recent years. The glorification of the "self-made" individual promotes the idea that personal achievement is solely the result of individual effort, often neglecting the role of community, support systems, and privilege. This narrative can lead to a lack of accountability and a diminished sense of responsibility for the impact of one's actions on others.

Additionally, the emphasis on self-expression can sometimes blur the lines between healthy self-advocacy and narcissism. While it is essential to honor one's identity and voice, the cultural push towards relentless self-promotion can encourage behaviors that prioritize self-interest over collaboration and understanding. As individuals become more focused on asserting their identities, they may inadvertently overlook the importance of fostering genuine connections and engaging with the perspectives of others.

Conclusion
In summary, the interplay of social media, consumerism, and evolving cultural values significantly shapes the landscape of narcissism in today's society. While self-centeredness may be increasingly normalized, it is essential to recognize the detrimental effects it can have on relationships and emotional well-being. By fostering awareness of these cultural influences, individuals can take steps to cultivate empathy, accountability, and a more balanced perspective on self-worth—ultimately leading to healthier interactions and a more connected society.

Chapter 2

Recognizing Narcissism in Yourself

Recognizing Narcissism in Yourself

Narcissism, while often perceived through a lens of grandiosity and self-importance, can manifest in various subtle and overt ways. Understanding the signs that you may be struggling with narcissistic traits is the first step towards self-awareness and healing. Here are some common indicators that might suggest narcissistic tendencies:

1. Excessive Need for Admiration: One hallmark of narcissism is an insatiable craving for validation and praise from others. If you find yourself constantly seeking compliments or feeling empty without external acknowledgments, this could be a significant red flag. It's not uncommon for individuals with narcissistic traits to feel a sense of worth that hinges on how others perceive them.

2. Sense of Entitlement: People exhibiting narcissistic traits often believe they deserve special treatment or that they are above the rules that govern others. This sense of entitlement may manifest in everyday interactions, such as expecting immediate responses to messages or feeling frustrated when plans do not cater to your preferences.

3. Lack of Empathy: An inability to empathize with others is a strong indicator of narcissism. If you struggle to recognize or validate the feelings and experiences of those around you, often prioritizing your needs and desires over theirs, it may suggest a disconnect from emotional understanding. This lack of emotional connection can lead to strained relationships and a cycle of misunderstanding.

4. Perfectionism and Unrealistic Standards: Narcissistic individuals frequently hold themselves—and others—to impossible standards. If you find yourself constantly striving for perfection and feeling inadequate when those standards aren't met, it can lead to feelings of shame and frustration. This behavior also extends to how you evaluate the accomplishments of others, often feeling envious or critical rather than supportive.

5. Defensiveness and Sensitivity to Criticism: A common trait among narcissists is a heightened sensitivity to criticism. If you find that you react defensively when receiving feedback—whether constructive or not—it may indicate a fragile self-esteem that you compensate for with narcissistic tendencies. This defensiveness often leads to a cycle of denial, making it difficult to acknowledge personal flaws or areas for growth.

6. Overemphasis on Self: If conversations consistently revolve around your achievements, opinions, and experiences, with little room for others to share their stories, this self-centeredness might suggest narcissism. Narcissistic individuals often struggle to engage in reciprocal conversations, leading to relationships that feel one-sided.

7. Difficulty in Maintaining Relationships: Relationships can often suffer due to narcissistic behaviors. Patterns of manipulation, lack of reciprocity, or emotional unavailability can create significant rifts in personal connections. If you frequently find yourself in conflict with friends, family, or romantic partners over issues of control or validation, it may be time to reflect on your relational dynamics.

8. Envy and Competition: Narcissistic individuals often feel envious of others' successes while simultaneously believing that others are envious of them. If you tend to view the achievements of others through a lens of jealousy rather than admiration or inspiration, this could signify underlying narcissistic traits.

9. Fear of Being Ordinary: There may be a deep-seated fear of being perceived as average or unremarkable. If the thought of mediocrity causes significant anxiety or dread, leading you to go to great lengths to stand out, this fear can be reflective of narcissistic tendencies.

Recognizing these signs in oneself can be a challenging yet transformative process. It requires honest self-reflection and a willingness to confront uncomfortable truths. Acknowledging these tendencies is not about self-judgment but rather about embarking on a path toward healthier self-awareness, empathy, and genuine connection with others. Embracing this awareness is the first step toward personal growth and healing, paving the way for a more fulfilling and empathetic life.

Common Patterns of Narcissistic Thoughts and Behaviors

Narcissism is not merely a personality trait but a complex behavioral pattern that manifests in various ways, impacting thoughts, emotions, and relationships. Understanding these patterns is crucial for those seeking to navigate the complexities of narcissistic behavior, whether in themselves or in others. This section explores the most prevalent patterns associated with narcissism, including perfectionism, a need for admiration, entitlement, and a lack of empathy.

Perfectionism
One of the most defining characteristics of narcissism is a relentless pursuit of perfection.

Narcissists often set unrealistically high standards for themselves and others, believing that anything less than perfect is unacceptable. This perfectionism serves multiple purposes: it provides a shield against feelings of inadequacy and allows narcissists to maintain an inflated self-image. When their expectations are not met, they may respond with anger, frustration, or withdrawal. This behavior not only perpetuates their self-centered view but also creates a toxic environment for those around them, leading to feelings of inadequacy and frustration in relationships.

Need for Admiration
A profound and often insatiable need for admiration is another hallmark of narcissistic behavior. Narcissists thrive on external validation, seeking constant praise and attention to reinforce their self-worth. This need can manifest in various ways, such as boasting about achievements, exaggerating accomplishments, or fishing for compliments. When they do not receive the admiration they seek, narcissists may react with rage or dejection, viewing the lack of attention as a personal affront. This pattern not only alienates others but also fosters an environment where relationships are transactional rather than genuine.

Entitlement
Narcissists frequently exhibit a strong sense of entitlement, believing they inherently deserve special treatment and privileges. This entitlement can lead to unreasonable expectations regarding how they should be treated by others, whether in personal relationships or professional settings. They may assume that others will prioritize their needs and desires above all else, often disregarding the feelings and needs of those around them. This pattern can result in significant conflict, as narcissists may react with anger or disdain when their expectations are not met, further entrenching their isolation.

Lack of Empathy
Perhaps the most damaging pattern associated with narcissism is a pronounced lack of empathy. Narcissists often struggle to recognize or value the emotions and experiences of others, leading to superficial and self-serving relationships. This deficit in empathy can manifest in various ways, such as dismissing the feelings of others, being unable to celebrate someone else's success, or failing to provide support in times of need. This lack of emotional connection can create a cycle of loneliness and resentment, both for the narcissist and those around them.

Other Patterns
In addition to these primary traits, narcissistic individuals may exhibit various other behaviors, including manipulation, gaslighting, and a tendency to devalue others. They often use these tactics to maintain control and reinforce their self-image, further complicating interactions and

relationships.

Conclusion
Recognizing these common patterns of narcissistic thoughts and behaviors is essential for both self-awareness and relational health. Individuals exhibiting narcissistic traits can benefit from understanding how these behaviors impact their lives and the lives of those around them. By identifying and addressing these patterns, it becomes possible to foster healthier relationships and encourage personal growth. Whether through self-reflection, therapy, or support from loved ones, acknowledging these traits is a crucial first step toward healing and transformation.

The Impact of Narcissism on Relationships
Narcissism, characterized by an exaggerated sense of self-importance, a constant need for admiration, and a lack of empathy, can significantly affect personal relationships. Understanding the impact of narcissism is essential for both those who may exhibit these traits and those who find themselves entangled with narcissistic individuals.

1. Erosion of Trust and Authenticity:
Narcissistic individuals often manipulate situations to maintain their self-image, leading to dishonesty and insincerity. This lack of authenticity can erode trust in relationships. Partners may feel deceived or invalidated when their concerns are dismissed or when their emotions are trivialized. Over time, this pattern of behavior can create an environment in which honesty is compromised, making it difficult for either party to feel secure in the relationship.

2. Emotional Rollercoaster:
Relationships with narcissistic individuals can resemble an emotional rollercoaster, marked by highs and lows. Initially, they may charm and idealize their partner, presenting an image of perfection and admiration that can be intoxicating. However, as the relationship progresses, their need for validation and admiration can lead to cycles of devaluation and withdrawal. Partners often find themselves feeling confused and anxious, trying to navigate the unpredictable emotional landscape that narcissism creates.

3. Lack of Empathy:
One of the most profound impacts of narcissism on relationships is the narcissist's inability to empathize. This emotional disconnect prevents them from understanding their partner's feelings, needs, or concerns. Consequently, partners may feel neglected, dismissed, or even invisible. This lack of empathy not only hurts the emotional bond but can also result in significant mental health repercussions for partners, including feelings of worthlessness, depression, and anxiety.

4. Codependency and Enabling:
Narcissistic relationships often lead to codependency, where the non-narcissistic partner may feel compelled to cater to the narcissist's needs at the expense of their own well-being. This dynamic not only reinforces the narcissist's behavior but also perpetuates an unhealthy cycle where the non-narcissistic partner feels trapped, unable to assert their boundaries or express their needs. This codependency can stifle personal growth and lead to long-term emotional distress.

5. Isolation and Alienation:
Narcissistic individuals often seek to control their partner's social interactions, leading to isolation and alienation from friends and family. The narcissist may undermine relationships with others through manipulation, fostering distrust and tension. This isolation can further entrench the non-narcissistic partner in the toxic dynamics of the relationship, making it even harder to seek support or perspective from outside sources.

6. Difficulty in Conflict Resolution:
Conflict resolution in relationships involving narcissistic individuals can be particularly challenging. Narcissists often react defensively to criticism or perceived slights, escalating conflicts instead of resolving them. Their tendency to dismiss or belittle their partner's feelings can create a hostile environment where healthy communication is virtually impossible. This can result in unresolved issues that fester and escalate over time, contributing to further discord.

7. Long-Term Consequences:
The long-term consequences of engaging in a relationship with a narcissistic individual can be severe. Partners may experience chronic stress, emotional instability, and a diminished sense of self-worth. Over time, the cumulative effects can lead to significant mental health issues, including anxiety disorders, depression, and post-traumatic stress.

In conclusion, the impact of narcissism on relationships is profound and multifaceted. Recognizing these dynamics is crucial for individuals either exhibiting narcissistic traits or those affected by them. Healthy relationships are built on trust, empathy, and mutual respect—qualities that narcissism fundamentally undermines. Understanding these impacts can empower individuals to seek the necessary changes for healing and growth, whether that involves setting boundaries, seeking therapy, or, in some cases, leaving toxic relationships altogether.

Self-Reflection and Accountability: Beginning Your Healing Journey
Embarking on a journey of healing from narcissistic traits is a profound and often challenging

undertaking. At its core, this journey is rooted in self-reflection and accountability—two essential components that can facilitate meaningful personal growth and transformation.

The Importance of Self-Reflection

Self-reflection is the practice of introspecting about one's thoughts, feelings, and behaviors. It involves critically examining the impact of one's actions on oneself and others, and it serves as the foundation for understanding the motivations behind narcissistic tendencies. Engaging in self-reflection allows individuals to identify patterns of thought and behavior that may be harmful, not only to themselves but also to those around them.

To begin this process, setting aside dedicated time for introspection is crucial. This could involve journaling about daily experiences, emotions, and triggers that elicit narcissistic responses. Questions such as "What emotions do I feel when I receive criticism?" or "How do my actions affect the people I care about?" can guide this exploration. The goal is to foster an honest and compassionate dialogue with oneself, recognizing both strengths and areas for improvement without judgment.

Understanding Accountability

Accountability is about taking responsibility for one's actions and their consequences. It entails recognizing that while narcissistic traits may have been formed as a means of coping with underlying vulnerabilities, it is ultimately the individual's responsibility to address these behaviors and their impacts. Accountability means acknowledging harmful actions, learning from them, and committing to change.

An effective way to cultivate accountability is to establish personal goals related to overcoming narcissism. These goals should be specific, measurable, achievable, relevant, and time-bound (SMART). For instance, one might set a goal to practice active listening during conversations, aiming to improve empathy and reduce self-centeredness. Tracking progress towards these goals can foster a sense of ownership and motivate continued effort.

Building a Support System

As self-reflection and accountability unfold, surrounding oneself with supportive individuals becomes vital. Sharing the journey with trusted friends, family members, or a therapist can provide valuable feedback, encouragement, and perspective. These relationships can help individuals stay grounded and motivated, especially during challenging times when old habits may resurface.

Group therapy can also be particularly beneficial. It creates a safe environment where individuals can share experiences, learn from others, and develop essential interpersonal skills. Hearing the stories of others struggling with similar issues can foster a sense of community and reduce feelings of isolation.

Embracing Vulnerability
A significant aspect of healing from narcissistic traits involves embracing vulnerability. This means allowing oneself to feel uncomfortable emotions such as shame, guilt, or sadness without immediately reacting defensively or seeking external validation. Acknowledging these feelings is crucial to breaking the cycle of narcissistic behavior.

Practicing vulnerability can be as simple as sharing one's struggles with a trusted person or admitting when one is wrong. Learning to apologize sincerely and seeking forgiveness can be a powerful step toward rebuilding trust in relationships that may have been damaged by narcissistic tendencies.

The Path Forward
As individuals engage in self-reflection and accountability, they will likely encounter both successes and setbacks. It is essential to approach this journey with self-compassion, recognizing that change takes time and effort. Celebrating small victories along the way can reinforce positive behaviors, while setbacks should be viewed as opportunities for learning rather than failures.

Ultimately, beginning the healing journey from narcissism requires a commitment to self-awareness, responsibility, and growth. By embracing self-reflection and accountability, individuals can cultivate healthier relationships, develop greater empathy, and foster a more authentic and fulfilling life. Through this transformative process, they can begin to break free from the confines of narcissism and embark on a path toward emotional well-being and connection with others.

Recognizing Defensiveness: How to Overcome Denial
Defensiveness is a common psychological response, especially among individuals exhibiting narcissistic traits. It serves as a protective mechanism against perceived threats, criticism, or feelings of inadequacy. Understanding and recognizing defensiveness is crucial for personal growth and overcoming denial, which often hinders emotional healing and relationship-building.

Understanding Defensiveness
Defensiveness manifests in various forms, including denial, rationalization, blame-shifting, and

emotional outbursts. When confronted with criticism, a defensively inclined individual might dismiss the feedback entirely, rationalize their actions, or project blame onto others. This behavior creates a barrier to self-reflection and personal accountability, perpetuating a cycle of unresolved issues and relationship struggles.

One of the significant challenges of defensiveness is the difficulty it poses in acknowledging one's flaws or mistakes. This denial is often rooted in a deep fear of vulnerability, rejection, and exposure. For individuals with narcissistic tendencies, admitting to shortcomings can feel like a threat to their self-image, leading to an instinctive, defensive reaction.

Recognizing Your Defensiveness
The first step in overcoming defensiveness is to cultivate self-awareness. Here are some signs that you may be exhibiting defensiveness:

1. Immediate Reactions: If you find yourself reacting quickly to criticism with anger or dismissal, this might indicate defensiveness.

2. Rationalization: Frequently justifying your actions or decisions without considering alternative viewpoints can be a defense mechanism.

3. Blame Shifting: If you often point fingers at others when faced with feedback, this is a clear sign of avoiding accountability.

4. Emotional Outbursts: Intense emotional reactions, such as frustration or withdrawal, in response to perceived criticism reflect a defensive stance.

Recognizing these patterns is essential in beginning the process of change. Journaling can be an effective tool to track your reactions and reflect on instances where defensiveness arises. Over time, this practice can help you identify triggers and patterns in your behavior.

Strategies to Overcome Defensiveness

1. Practice Mindfulness: Developing mindfulness can help you become more aware of your emotional triggers. Mindfulness encourages a non-judgmental observation of thoughts and feelings, enabling you to pause before reacting defensively. Deep breathing exercises and meditation can aid in cultivating this awareness.

2. Embrace Vulnerability: Understanding that vulnerability is not a weakness but a strength is crucial in overcoming defensiveness. Allow yourself to be open to feedback and recognize that everyone makes mistakes. This mindset shift fosters a more compassionate view of yourself and others.

3. Seek Feedback: Actively seek constructive criticism from trusted friends or family. Create a safe space for open dialogue where you invite honest feedback. This practice not only helps in reducing defensiveness but also strengthens relationships through mutual understanding and respect.

4. Develop Emotional Regulation Skills: Learning to manage your emotional responses is vital. When you feel defensive, take a moment to breathe deeply and assess the situation. Ask yourself whether your reaction is proportionate to the feedback received. This pause can prevent impulsive responses and foster more thoughtful communication.

5. Apologize and Reflect: When you recognize defensiveness in your behavior, acknowledge it. If your defensiveness has hurt someone, a sincere apology can go a long way. Reflect on the situation to understand why you reacted defensively and how you can respond differently in the future.

Conclusion

Overcoming defensiveness is a crucial step in the journey toward healing from narcissistic traits and fostering healthier relationships. By developing self-awareness, embracing vulnerability, seeking feedback, and honing emotional regulation skills, you can break free from the cycle of denial. This transformation not only enhances personal growth but also enriches your connections with others, leading to a more authentic and fulfilling life.

Chapter 3

Narcissism and Relationships

The Role of Narcissism in Personal Relationships

Narcissism, characterized by self-centeredness, a lack of empathy, and an excessive need for admiration, can profoundly affect personal relationships across various contexts, including romantic partnerships, family dynamics, and friendships. Understanding how narcissism manifests in these relationships is crucial for fostering healthier interactions and mitigating the potential damage that narcissistic behaviors can inflict.

Romantic Relationships

In romantic settings, narcissism can create a toxic imbalance. Individuals with narcissistic tendencies often engage in idealization followed by devaluation—a cycle that can leave their partners feeling confused and emotionally drained. Initially, the narcissistic partner may shower their significant other with affection and attention, creating a sense of euphoria. However, as the relationship progresses, they may begin to withdraw affection, criticize, or belittle their partner, often projecting their insecurities onto them. This pattern can lead to emotional abuse, where the non-narcissistic partner feels trapped in a cycle of seeking validation and love from someone who is inherently incapable of providing it.

The impact of narcissism in romantic relationships extends beyond emotional distress; it can also lead to significant issues such as codependency. Partners of narcissists may sacrifice their own needs and desires to maintain the relationship, ultimately losing their sense of self. Conversely, narcissists may struggle to maintain long-term, meaningful connections due to their inability to empathize and engage in mutual vulnerability, which are essential for healthy intimacy.

Family Dynamics

Narcissism in family relationships can be particularly damaging, as familial bonds often create a complex web of expectations, responsibilities, and emotional entanglements. Narcissistic parents may place unrealistic demands on their children, expecting them to fulfill their own unmet needs for validation and success. This can lead to a range of outcomes, from anxiety and low self-esteem in children to strained family relationships. Children raised in narcissistic households may internalize the belief that their worth is tied to their ability to please others, leading to difficulties in asserting themselves and establishing healthy boundaries later in life.

Siblings of narcissistic individuals may also experience emotional neglect or rivalry, as the narcissist often seeks to be the center of attention, undermining the achievements and feelings of others. This can create a household atmosphere rife with competition and resentment, hindering the development of supportive and nurturing familial bonds.

Friendships

In friendships, narcissism can manifest as a one-sided relationship where the narcissistic individual dominates conversations, seeks constant validation, and often fails to offer support in return. Friends may find themselves in a perpetual state of emotional labor, where their own needs are sidelined in favor of the narcissist's need for admiration and attention. Over time, this can lead to a breakdown of trust and mutual respect, as genuine connections are overshadowed by the narcissist's self-serving behaviors.

Moreover, narcissism can lead to social isolation for both the narcissist and their friends. The narcissist's inability to form authentic connections can alienate them from their social circles, while friends may distance themselves to protect their emotional well-being. This isolation can perpetuate the narcissist's cycle of seeking validation through superficial relationships, further entrenching their self-centered behaviors.

Conclusion

Recognizing the role of narcissism in personal relationships is essential for fostering healthier connections. Whether in romantic partnerships, family structures, or friendships, the consequences of narcissistic behavior can be profound and long-lasting. By understanding these dynamics, individuals can take proactive steps to establish boundaries, seek support, and promote emotional health, ultimately leading to more fulfilling and empathetic relationships. Emphasizing self-awareness and accountability is vital for both narcissists and their loved ones, paving the way for healing and growth.

How Narcissism Can Lead to Toxic Patterns

Narcissism, characterized by an inflated sense of self-importance and a deep need for admiration, can create a multitude of toxic patterns in interpersonal relationships. These patterns often manifest in behaviors that not only affect the narcissist but also have far-reaching consequences on those around them, leading to a cycle of dysfunction that can be difficult to break.

1. Manipulation and Control

One of the hallmark traits of narcissistic behavior is the tendency to manipulate and control others. Narcissists often employ tactics such as gaslighting, guilt-tripping, and emotional blackmail to maintain their desired level of control. This manipulation can erode the self-esteem of those around them, fostering a sense of dependency that keeps individuals tethered to the narcissist. For example, a narcissistic partner may undermine their significant other's self-worth, convincing them that they are incapable of making decisions without their guidance. This toxic dynamic can lead to feelings of confusion, anxiety, and self-doubt in the victim.

2. Lack of Accountability
Narcissists typically exhibit a profound inability to take responsibility for their actions. When confronted with their behavior, they often deflect blame onto others or minimize the impact of their actions. This lack of accountability can create a toxic environment where individuals feel compelled to walk on eggshells to avoid triggering a defensive reaction. Over time, this leads to resentment and frustration among those affected, as they may feel their feelings and experiences are invalidated or ignored.

3. Intermittent Reinforcement
Narcissists frequently engage in a behavior known as intermittent reinforcement, wherein they alternate between offering affection and withdrawing it. This inconsistency can create a psychological and emotional rollercoaster for those involved, leading them to cling to the moments of validation when the narcissist is at their best, while enduring the pain of their more toxic behaviors. This pattern can create a false sense of hope and an unhealthy attachment, making it difficult for individuals to break free from the cycle of abuse.

4. Isolation from Support Systems
Another toxic pattern associated with narcissism is the tendency to isolate individuals from their support networks. A narcissist may attempt to sever ties with friends and family, creating a sense of dependency on the relationship. This isolation not only enhances control but also deprives the victim of external perspectives that could help them recognize the toxicity of the relationship. When individuals are cut off from their support systems, they may become more entrenched in the narcissistic dynamic, feeling unable to escape.

5. Emotional Turmoil and Resentment
Living with or being in a relationship with a narcissist can lead to significant emotional turmoil. Individuals often experience feelings of anger, resentment, and helplessness as they grapple with the narcissist's erratic behavior. This emotional distress can manifest in various ways, including anxiety, depression, and even physical health issues. Over time, the cumulative effect of this emotional toll can create a toxic atmosphere that affects not just the individual but also the relationships they hold.

6. Cycle of Narcissistic Abuse
The interplay of these toxic patterns often leads to a vicious cycle of narcissistic abuse. Victims may find themselves caught in an endless loop of seeking validation from the narcissist, experiencing manipulation, and then withdrawing due to the emotional toll. This cycle can perpetuate unhealthy dynamics, making it essential for individuals to recognize these patterns and seek help in breaking free.

In conclusion, narcissism can lead to toxic patterns that not only harm the narcissist but also devastate relationships and the well-being of those they affect. Recognizing these patterns is the first step towards healing and establishing healthier dynamics, both within oneself and in relationships with others. Through self-reflection and accountability, individuals can begin to break the cycle of narcissistic behavior and foster healthier, more empathetic connections.

Learning to Recognize Empathy Deficits in Yourself
Empathy, the ability to understand and share the feelings of others, is a crucial component of healthy interpersonal relationships. For individuals with narcissistic tendencies, empathy deficits can significantly impair their ability to connect with others, often leading to misunderstandings, conflict, and emotional distance. Recognizing these deficits is the first step toward personal growth and healing. Here, we will explore how to identify empathy deficits within oneself and the implications of these deficits on personal relationships.

Understanding Empathy Deficits
Empathy can be categorized into two main types: cognitive and emotional. Cognitive empathy refers to the ability to understand another person's perspective or mental state, while emotional empathy involves the capacity to feel and respond to another person's emotional experience. Narcissism often skews both forms of empathy, leading individuals to struggle with recognizing or valuing the feelings of those around them. This disconnect can manifest in various ways, including a lack of concern for others' emotions and an inability to respond appropriately to emotional cues.

Signs of Empathy Deficits

1. Difficulty Identifying Emotions: One of the first signs of an empathy deficit is a challenge in recognizing your own emotions or the emotions of others. If you find yourself often unsure of how others are feeling, or if you frequently misinterpret their emotional expressions, this may indicate a disconnect in your empathetic responses.

2. Self-Centered Conversations: If you notice that your conversations often revolve around your experiences, achievements, or problems without allowing space for the other person's inputs or feelings, it can be a sign of empathy deficits. A healthy dialogue should include active listening and an exchange of feelings, rather than a one-sided narrative.

3. Minimal Emotional Response: Assess how you react when someone shares their struggles or heartaches. If your response tends to be dismissive or if you find it hard to express compassion, it may reveal an inability to connect emotionally with others. People with empathy deficits often struggle to feel moved by others' misfortunes, which can be mistaken for a lack of interest or care.

4. Avoiding Vulnerability: An aversion to vulnerability can also indicate empathy deficits. If you find yourself consistently avoiding discussions about emotions—both yours and others'—it may be a defense mechanism to protect your own ego. This avoidance can prevent you from forming deeper emotional connections with those around you.

5. Judgmental Attitudes: Narcissistic tendencies often lead to a critical or judgmental view of others. If you frequently find yourself blaming others for their problems or viewing their emotions as weaknesses, it may be an indicator of a lack of empathy. Recognizing that everyone has their struggles can help foster a more compassionate viewpoint.

Self-Reflection and Growth

To address empathy deficits, engaging in self-reflection is essential. This involves taking the time to evaluate your thoughts, feelings, and behaviors in relation to others. Journaling can be a powerful tool for this process, allowing you to articulate your feelings and recognize patterns in your emotional responses. Additionally, actively seeking feedback from trusted friends or family can provide insights into how your behavior impacts those around you.

Practicing mindfulness can also enhance emotional awareness. Mindfulness encourages you to stay present in interactions, allowing for a deeper understanding of others' emotions. By being fully attentive, you can cultivate greater empathy and learn to respond more appropriately to the feelings of others.

Conclusion

Learning to recognize empathy deficits within yourself is a fundamental step toward personal growth and healthier relationships. By acknowledging these deficits and actively working to address them, you can foster deeper connections, enhance your emotional intelligence, and ultimately lead a more fulfilling life. Cultivating empathy not only benefits your relationships but also contributes to your overall emotional well-being, creating a positive feedback loop of compassion and connection.

Building Healthy Boundaries in Relationships

Establishing healthy boundaries is essential for fostering relationships that are respectful, supportive, and nurturing. Boundaries define the limits of what is acceptable behavior from others while also clarifying what you are willing to accept in your interactions. They serve as a protective mechanism that allows individuals to maintain their sense of self, emotional safety, and personal well-being. Here, we will explore the importance of boundaries, how to set them without guilt, and the significance of recognizing and respecting the boundaries of others.

Understanding the Importance of Boundaries

Boundaries are crucial in any relationship, whether romantic, familial, or platonic. They help to:

1. Protect Emotional Well-Being: By defining what behaviors are acceptable, you safeguard yourself from emotional harm. Without boundaries, individuals may find themselves in toxic situations that erode their self-esteem and mental health.

2. Promote Respect and Trust: Healthy boundaries encourage respect between individuals. When both parties understand each other's limits, trust grows, fostering a safe space for open communication.

3. Enhance Personal Growth: Setting boundaries allows individuals to prioritize their needs and interests, which is essential for personal development. It creates an environment where one can flourish without feeling overwhelmed by the demands of others.

4. Improve Relationship Dynamics: Clear boundaries help to prevent misunderstandings and resentment, which can lead to conflict. When both parties know what to expect from each other, relationships tend to be more harmonious.

Setting Personal Boundaries Without Guilt

Many individuals struggle with the idea of setting boundaries due to feelings of guilt or fear of rejection. However, it is vital to remember that establishing boundaries is not an act of selfishness; rather, it is a necessary step towards maintaining a healthy relationship. Here's how to set personal boundaries:

1. Reflect on Your Needs: Assess your emotional and physical needs to determine what boundaries are necessary for your well-being. Consider past experiences where you felt uncomfortable or violated, as these can inform what boundaries you need to establish.

2. Communicate Clearly: When discussing your boundaries with others, be direct and assertive. Use "I" statements to express your feelings and explain your needs without sounding accusatory. For example, "I feel overwhelmed when plans change at the last minute, so I need advance notice."

3. Be Consistent: Boundaries require consistency to be effective. If you set a boundary, it's crucial to uphold it. Consistency helps reinforce the message that your needs are valid and must be respected.

4. Practice Self-Compassion: Recognize that setting boundaries may cause discomfort initially, both for you and others. Allow yourself to feel that discomfort without judgment and remind yourself that your needs and feelings are important.

Recognizing and Respecting the Boundaries of Others

Just as you have needs and limits, so do others. Respecting the boundaries set by others is fundamental to healthy relationships. Here are some ways to ensure you are honoring the boundaries of those around you:

1. Listen Actively: When someone expresses their boundaries, listen attentively without interrupting. Validate their feelings and acknowledge their right to set limits.

2. Avoid Assumptions: Never assume you know what someone else needs or wants. Always ask for clarification if you are uncertain about their boundaries, and be open to their responses.

3. Apologize When Necessary: If you unintentionally cross someone's boundary, acknowledge the mistake and apologize. This demonstrates respect for their feelings and a commitment to improving your relationship.

4. Encourage Open Dialogue: Foster an environment where both parties feel safe to express their needs and boundaries. Encourage discussions about boundaries regularly, allowing for adjustments as relationships evolve.

In conclusion, building healthy boundaries in relationships is a critical component of emotional wellness and interpersonal harmony. By understanding the importance of boundaries, learning to set them without guilt, and respecting the boundaries of others, individuals can create relationships that are supportive, balanced, and fulfilling. Ultimately, healthy boundaries empower us to engage with others while maintaining our individuality and integrity.

Repairing Relationships Damaged by Narcissistic Behavior

Repairing relationships affected by narcissistic behavior is a complex and often challenging process. Narcissism can create deep emotional wounds, which may lead to feelings of betrayal, resentment, and disconnect. However, with commitment, self-awareness, and the right strategies, it is possible to mend these relationships and cultivate a healthier dynamic. Here are key steps to consider when embarking on this journey:

1. Acknowledge the Damage:
The first step in repairing a relationship is acknowledging the impact of narcissistic behavior. This means recognizing how actions—whether manipulative, dismissive, or self-centered—have affected the other person. It is crucial for the narcissistic individual to take responsibility for their actions without deflecting blame or minimizing the hurt caused. This acknowledgment is fundamental in rebuilding trust and demonstrates a willingness to change.

2. Practice Genuine Apologies:
An effective apology goes beyond mere words; it must be sincere and demonstrate an understanding of the pain inflicted. A genuine apology includes acknowledging the specific behaviors that caused harm, expressing remorse, and committing to change. This process not only allows the injured party to feel heard but also fosters a sense of accountability in the individual seeking to repair the relationship.

3. Commit to Self-Reflection:
Self-reflection is an essential tool for anyone seeking to repair relationships damaged by narcissism. This involves examining one's thoughts, feelings, and behaviors to understand their motivations and triggers. By engaging in self-reflection, individuals can better comprehend how their narcissistic traits manifest and how these traits affect their relationships. Keeping a journal can be particularly beneficial in tracking personal growth and identifying patterns that need addressing.

4. Establish Open Communication:
Effective communication is vital for healing. This means not only expressing one's feelings in a constructive manner but also actively listening to the concerns of the other person. The narcissistic individual should create a safe space for open dialogue, allowing the other person to express their feelings and experiences without fear of judgment or retaliation. Listening with empathy and validating their feelings can significantly strengthen the relationship.

5. Set Boundaries:
Healthy boundaries are essential in any relationship, especially when recovering from narcissistic behavior. Both parties should discuss and establish clear boundaries that protect their emotional well-being. For the individual with narcissistic tendencies, this may involve recognizing their limits and respecting the needs and boundaries of others. Conversely, the injured party should feel empowered to articulate their boundaries without guilt.

6. Cultivate Empathy:
Developing empathy is crucial in repairing relationships impacted by narcissism. This involves striving to understand the other person's perspective and acknowledging their feelings. Practicing empathy can be enhanced through active listening, engaging in perspective-taking exercises, and fostering compassion within oneself. These practices can help bridge the emotional gap that narcissism often creates.

7. Engage in Therapeutic Support:
Professional help can be invaluable in repairing relationships affected by narcissistic behavior. Individual or couple's therapy can provide tools and strategies for healing, enhancing communication, and managing emotional responses. A therapist can guide both partners through the complexities of their emotional landscape, helping them navigate the challenges of rebuilding trust and connection.

8. Commit to Continuous Growth:
Repairing relationships is not a one-time event but an ongoing process that requires dedication and effort. Both individuals should commit to personal growth and ongoing self-awareness, recognizing that change takes time. Celebrating small victories along the way can reinforce positive behaviors and strengthen the bond between partners.

In conclusion, while repairing relationships damaged by narcissistic behavior can be a daunting task, it is achievable through commitment, empathy, and open communication. By acknowledging past mistakes, practicing genuine apologies, and establishing healthy boundaries, individuals can foster a more authentic and fulfilling connection with one another. Ultimately, the journey to healing requires patience, consistent effort, and a willingness to grow together.

Chapter 4

The Narcissism-Empathy Disconnect

Understanding Empathy: Cognitive vs. Emotional Empathy

Empathy plays a crucial role in human relationships, serving as the foundation for connection, understanding, and compassion. The concept of empathy can be divided into two primary types: cognitive empathy and emotional empathy. While both forms contribute to our ability to relate to others, they manifest in distinct ways and have different implications for interpersonal dynamics.

Cognitive Empathy

Cognitive empathy refers to the ability to understand another person's perspective, thoughts, and feelings without necessarily sharing those emotions. It involves the mental capacity to recognize and comprehend what someone else is experiencing. This form of empathy is often described as "perspective-taking" and is closely linked to intellectual understanding.

Individuals with strong cognitive empathy can accurately assess the emotional states of others and predict how they might react in various situations. For instance, a manager in a workplace may utilize cognitive empathy to gauge how an employee might feel about a new policy change, enabling them to communicate that change more effectively.

While cognitive empathy is invaluable for problem-solving and navigating complex social situations, it can sometimes lead to a disconnection between understanding and emotional engagement. A person may intellectually grasp what someone else is going through but fail to feel compassion or concern. This dispassionate understanding can result in a lack of genuine connection, as emotional resonance is essential for fostering deeper relationships.

Emotional Empathy

Emotional empathy, on the other hand, is the ability to physically feel what another person is experiencing. This form of empathy allows individuals to resonate with others' emotional states on a visceral level, often leading to emotional reactions that mirror those of the other person. For example, witnessing a friend who is grieving may elicit feelings of sadness and sorrow within oneself, creating a shared emotional experience.

Emotional empathy plays a critical role in nurturing compassionate responses and fostering strong interpersonal bonds. It encourages individuals to offer support, comfort, and validation to others, as they not only understand the other's perspective but also feel their pain or joy. This deep emotional connection can be particularly beneficial in relationships, as it creates a sense of safety and belonging.

However, emotional empathy can also present challenges. For those who are highly sensitive, taking on the emotional weight of others can lead to emotional burnout or compassion fatigue. It can be difficult to maintain a balance between feeling deeply for others while also protecting one's emotional well-being.

The Interplay Between Cognitive and Emotional Empathy

Both cognitive and emotional empathy are essential for healthy relationships. They often work in tandem: cognitive empathy allows individuals to understand a situation from another's viewpoint, while emotional empathy promotes a genuine emotional connection. When both forms are present, individuals can engage in meaningful conversations, offer appropriate support, and cultivate a deeper understanding of one another.

However, the narcissism-empathy disconnect can create barriers to this dual empathy experience. Narcissistic individuals may excel in cognitive empathy, using their understanding to manipulate or control situations rather than to connect meaningfully. Conversely, they often struggle with emotional empathy, leading to a lack of genuine compassion for others.

In conclusion, understanding the distinction between cognitive and emotional empathy is vital for developing healthier relationships and fostering emotional intelligence. By enhancing both forms of empathy, individuals can work toward greater connection, compassion, and understanding, ultimately leading to more fulfilling interactions and a richer emotional life. Emphasizing the cultivation of both types of empathy may serve as a transformative step toward healing narcissistic traits and building authentic connections with others.

Why Narcissism Blocks True Empathy

Empathy is the capacity to understand and share the feelings of others. It forms the foundation of meaningful connections, fostering compassion and emotional support. However, narcissism, characterized by a pervasive pattern of grandiosity, need for admiration, and a lack of empathy, fundamentally obstructs this critical emotional skill. Understanding why narcissism blocks true empathy requires delving into the psychological mechanisms underpinning narcissistic behavior and the nature of empathy itself.

The Nature of Narcissism

Narcissism can be viewed as a defense mechanism rooted in deep-seated insecurities.

Individuals with narcissistic traits often present an inflated self-image to the world, masking vulnerabilities and fears of inadequacy. This self-focus creates a barrier to engaging with the emotional experiences of others. When one is preoccupied with self-importance and validation, the ability to tune into the feelings and needs of others diminishes significantly.

Cognitive vs. Emotional Empathy
Empathy is typically categorized into two types: cognitive empathy and emotional empathy. Cognitive empathy refers to the ability to understand another person's perspective and feelings, while emotional empathy involves sharing and resonating with those feelings on a deeper emotional level. Narcissistic individuals may exhibit a degree of cognitive empathy; they can often recognize what others are feeling or thinking but struggle to connect with those feelings emotionally. This disconnect arises because their focus remains primarily on their own needs and experiences, leaving little room for genuine emotional engagement with others.

The Role of Self-Centeredness
Narcissism encourages a self-centered worldview where the individual prioritizes their own needs and desires above all else. This self-absorption limits awareness of others' emotions and experiences. In relationships, narcissistic individuals may engage in conversations that revolve around their achievements or problems, providing little space for others to express themselves. Such interactions reinforce a cycle where the narcissist's need for admiration overshadows the potential for empathy, rendering interactions superficial and often transactional.

Fear of Vulnerability
True empathy requires vulnerability—the willingness to connect with the feelings of others and to share one's own emotional experiences. Narcissistic individuals often fear vulnerability, perceiving it as a weakness that could be exploited. Their protective mechanisms lead them to avoid emotional connections that require authentic sharing and understanding. Instead, they may resort to superficial displays of sympathy that lack depth and authenticity, further obstructing the pathway to true empathy.

Defense Mechanisms and Emotional Disconnect
Narcissists frequently employ defense mechanisms such as denial, projection, and rationalization to protect their fragile self-esteem. These mechanisms create an emotional disconnect, making it difficult to genuinely engage with the emotional states of others. For instance, when faced with criticism or negative feedback, a narcissistic individual may deflect or project their insecurities onto the critic rather than reflecting on the feedback. This defensive posture reinforces their inability to empathize, as they remain entrenched in their self-centered narrative.

Cultural and Social Influences
In a society that often rewards individualism and self-promotion, narcissism can thrive, further entrenching the barriers to empathy. Social media platforms amplify this self-centeredness, encouraging individuals to curate a persona centered on admiration and validation. The constant need for external validation exacerbates the disconnect from authentic human experiences, as the focus shifts from genuine connections to superficial interactions.

Conclusion
Narcissism obstructs true empathy through self-absorption, fear of vulnerability, and reliance on defense mechanisms. This emotional barrier not only affects the narcissist's relationships but also contributes to a broader culture that undervalues authentic emotional engagement. Addressing these barriers is crucial for healing and fostering deeper connections, allowing individuals to reclaim the capacity for empathy that is vital for fulfilling relationships and emotional well-being.

Reconnecting with Empathy: Techniques for Developing Compassion
Empathy is the ability to understand and share the feelings of another, acting as a crucial bridge in building meaningful relationships and fostering emotional well-being. For individuals struggling with narcissistic traits, reconnecting with empathy can be a transformative journey. Developing compassion not only enhances interpersonal connections but also facilitates personal healing. Here are several techniques to cultivate empathy and compassion in one's life.

1. Practice Active Listening
Active listening is more than simply hearing words; it involves fully engaging with the speaker, both verbally and non-verbally. This technique requires setting aside distractions and genuinely focusing on what the other person is saying. When practicing active listening, one should maintain eye contact, nod in acknowledgment, and refrain from interrupting. After the speaker expresses their feelings, paraphrasing their message shows that you have understood them. This practice fosters a deeper connection and allows you to appreciate the speaker's perspective, which is foundational for empathetic engagement.

2. Engage in Perspective-Taking
Perspective-taking involves stepping into someone else's shoes and viewing situations from their point of view. This can be practiced by asking oneself questions such as, "How would I feel if I were in their situation?" or "What might they be experiencing emotionally?" Journaling can assist in this process by allowing individuals to articulate the thoughts and feelings of others, facilitating a deeper understanding of their experiences. Moreover, consuming diverse narratives through literature, films, or documentaries can expose individuals to different life

situations and emotions, broadening their empathetic capacity.

3. Cultivate Mindfulness
Mindfulness—the practice of being present in the moment—can significantly enhance one's capacity for empathy. By focusing on the present, individuals become more attuned to their own feelings and the emotions of those around them. Mindfulness exercises, such as meditation or deep-breathing techniques, can create a mental space where one can observe thoughts and emotions without judgment. This awareness helps in recognizing emotional cues in others, fostering a compassionate response rather than an automatic self-centered reaction.

4. Volunteer and Serve Others
Engaging in acts of service can be a powerful way to reconnect with empathy. Volunteering provides opportunities to interact with individuals from diverse backgrounds and experiences. This exposure can dismantle preconceived notions and foster a genuine understanding of different life challenges. The shared human experience of helping others can evoke feelings of compassion and reinforce the interconnectedness of humanity.

5. Reflect on Personal Emotions
Regular self-reflection is vital in understanding one's emotional responses and how they affect others. Keeping a journal that explores personal feelings, reactions, and interactions can help illuminate patterns of behavior that may be self-centered. This practice encourages individuals to consider how their actions impact others, promoting a shift towards a more empathetic mindset.

6. Develop Emotional Vocabulary
Understanding and articulating one's own emotions is key to developing empathy. Expanding emotional vocabulary helps in recognizing feelings in oneself and others. Instead of defaulting to generic terms like "happy" or "sad," individuals can learn to describe nuances such as "disappointed," "joyful," or "anxious." This deeper understanding enables more meaningful emotional exchanges and fosters compassionate interactions.

7. Seek Feedback
Asking for feedback from trusted friends or family members about how one's behavior affects others can provide invaluable insights. This feedback loop encourages accountability and fosters a greater understanding of how one's actions may be perceived. By being open to constructive criticism, individuals can make conscious efforts to adjust their behavior, enhancing their empathetic responses.

Conclusion

Reconnecting with empathy is a crucial step towards healing and personal growth for those grappling with narcissistic tendencies. By practicing active listening, engaging in perspective-taking, cultivating mindfulness, volunteering, reflecting on personal emotions, developing emotional vocabulary, and seeking feedback, individuals can foster compassion within themselves. This journey not only strengthens relationships but also enriches one's experience of life, promoting a deeper sense of connection with others. Ultimately, empathy lays the groundwork for healthier interactions and a more fulfilling existence, free from the constraints of self-centeredness.

Practicing Active Listening and Perspective-Taking

Active listening and perspective-taking are crucial skills in cultivating empathy and improving interpersonal relationships, particularly for individuals grappling with narcissistic tendencies. These skills not only foster understanding and connection but also facilitate personal growth and healing from self-centered behaviors. By honing these abilities, one can transform interactions, nurture deeper bonds, and ultimately lead a more fulfilling, narcissism-free life.

Understanding Active Listening

Active listening is a communication technique that involves fully concentrating, understanding, responding, and remembering what the other person is saying. It is essential to go beyond merely hearing words; instead, it requires engaging with the speaker both verbally and non-verbally. Key components of active listening include:

1. Attention: Focus entirely on the speaker, minimizing distractions. This means putting away phones, maintaining eye contact, and showing openness through body language.

2. Reflection: After the speaker shares their thoughts, paraphrase or summarize what they've said to demonstrate understanding. This not only shows that you are listening but also helps clarify any misunderstandings.

3. Validation: Acknowledge the speaker's feelings and perspectives without judgment. It's important to convey that their emotions are valid, even if you do not necessarily agree with their viewpoint.

4. Questions: Ask open-ended questions to encourage the speaker to elaborate on their thoughts and feelings. This demonstrates genuine interest and helps deepen the conversation.

5. Nonverbal Cues: Use appropriate body language, such as nodding, maintaining an open posture, and leaning slightly forward to indicate engagement and interest.

The Importance of Perspective-Taking

Perspective-taking goes hand in hand with active listening. It refers to the ability to view a situation from someone else's point of view, fostering empathy and understanding. This skill is particularly vital for individuals struggling with narcissism, as it counters self-centered thinking patterns. To develop effective perspective-taking skills, consider the following strategies:

1. Empathetic Imagination: When engaging with others, consciously try to imagine what they might be feeling or experiencing. Ask yourself how you would feel in their shoes, which can help bridge emotional gaps.

2. Avoid Assumptions: Refrain from jumping to conclusions about the speaker's thoughts or feelings. Instead, seek clarification and give them the space to express themselves fully.

3. Diverse Interactions: Engage with a variety of people from different backgrounds, cultures, and experiences. This exposure can broaden your understanding and appreciation of diverse viewpoints.

4. Mindfulness Practice: Use mindfulness techniques to become more aware of your own thoughts and feelings, which can help you separate your perspective from that of others. This awareness allows for a more genuine understanding of different viewpoints.

Benefits of Active Listening and Perspective-Taking

The practice of active listening and perspective-taking can yield numerous benefits, especially for individuals looking to heal from narcissistic traits. These benefits include:

- **Enhanced Relationships:** Improved communication fosters trust and connection, leading to healthier and more fulfilling relationships with family, friends, and colleagues.

- **Conflict Resolution:** By understanding different perspectives and validating emotions, individuals are better equipped to resolve conflicts amicably, reducing misunderstandings and hostility.

- **Emotional Growth:** Engaging with others in this way encourages self-reflection and introspection. It allows individuals to process their feelings and reactions, promoting emotional maturity.

- **Increased Empathy:** Regular practice of active listening and perspective-taking enhances one's capacity for empathy, reducing self-centeredness and fostering a more compassionate outlook on life.

In conclusion, practicing active listening and perspective-taking is vital for anyone seeking to overcome narcissistic tendencies and cultivate healthier interpersonal relationships. By committing to these practices, individuals can foster deeper connections, enhance their emotional intelligence, and embark on a transformative journey toward a more empathetic and fulfilling life.

How Cultivating Empathy Strengthens Relationships

Empathy is the ability to understand and share the feelings of another person. It is a fundamental component of healthy relationships, enabling individuals to connect on a deeper emotional level and fostering mutual understanding. In a world often characterized by self-centeredness, particularly in the context of narcissism, cultivating empathy becomes an essential skill for nurturing and sustaining meaningful connections with others.

The Role of Empathy in Relationships

At its core, empathy allows individuals to step into someone else's shoes, to perceive the world from their perspective. This ability is critical in interpersonal relationships, whether they are romantic, familial, or platonic. When we practice empathy, we demonstrate that we value the experiences and emotions of others, which in turn encourages openness and trust.

1. Enhanced Communication: Empathy facilitates better communication by allowing us to listen actively and respond thoughtfully. When we understand how someone else is feeling, we are less likely to react defensively and more likely to engage in constructive dialogue. This not only reduces conflict but also helps in resolving misunderstandings more effectively.

2. Emotional Support: Relationships thrive on emotional support. By cultivating empathy, we become more attuned to the struggles and needs of others. This heightened awareness enables us to provide appropriate support, whether it's a comforting word during a tough time or celebrating a friend's achievements. When individuals feel seen and supported, it strengthens their bond with us.

3. Conflict Resolution: Conflicts are a natural part of any relationship. However, empathy can significantly reduce the frequency and intensity of conflicts. When we approach disagreements with empathy, we are more inclined to see the situation from the other person's viewpoint. This perspective shift can lead to collaborative solutions that address the needs of both parties, transforming potential conflicts into opportunities for growth.

4. Building Trust: Trust is the foundation of any healthy relationship. When we demonstrate empathy, we show that we care about others' feelings and perspectives. This fosters a sense of safety, as people are more likely to open up and share their thoughts without fearing judgment. In contrast, a lack of empathy can lead to feelings of isolation and misunderstanding, damaging the trust that is essential for a strong relationship.

Techniques for Cultivating Empathy

Cultivating empathy is an active process that requires intentional practice. Here are some techniques that can help enhance empathetic skills:

- **Active Listening:** This involves giving full attention to the speaker, acknowledging their feelings, and responding with validation. By doing so, we convey that their experiences are important.

- **Perspective-Taking:** Challenge yourself to see situations from the viewpoints of others. Ask questions that dig deeper into their feelings and experiences, which can help clarify their emotions and reactions.

- **Mindfulness Practices:** Developing mindfulness can increase emotional awareness. Techniques such as meditation can help us become more present and attuned to our own feelings, which can enhance our ability to empathize with others.

- **Engagement with Diverse Perspectives:** Exposing ourselves to different cultures, experiences, and narratives can broaden our understanding of the human experience. This can be accomplished through reading, attending workshops, or engaging in community activities.

The Transformative Power of Empathy

Ultimately, cultivating empathy strengthens relationships by fostering a culture of respect, understanding, and support. As we become more empathetic, we not only enhance our connections with others but also contribute to a more compassionate and connected society. In doing so, we break down the barriers of narcissism and self-centeredness, creating a more harmonious and fulfilling existence for ourselves and those around us. By prioritizing empathy, we lay the groundwork for healthier, more resilient relationships that can withstand the tests of time and adversity.

Chapter 5

Breaking the Cycle of Narcissistic Behavior

Identifying the Core Fears Behind Narcissism

Understanding the core fears behind narcissism is crucial for recognizing the underlying issues that drive narcissistic behaviors. Despite the outward confidence and self-absorption often displayed by narcissists, these traits frequently mask deep-seated vulnerabilities. By identifying these fears, individuals can begin to unravel the complex web of narcissism and work toward healing.

Fear of Inadequacy

At the heart of many narcissistic behaviors lies a profound fear of inadequacy. Individuals with narcissistic tendencies often grapple with feelings of worthlessness or inferiority. This fear can stem from childhood experiences, where they may have faced criticism, neglect, or unrealistic expectations from caregivers. To compensate for these feelings, narcissists may present an exaggerated sense of self-importance and accomplishments, striving to convince themselves and others of their superiority.

Recognizing this fear is essential for personal growth. It allows individuals to challenge the narrative that they must always be exceptional to be worthy of love and respect. Accepting imperfections as part of being human can help dismantle the facade of superiority and foster genuine self-acceptance.

Fear of Abandonment

Another core fear often associated with narcissism is the fear of abandonment. Narcissists may have experienced unstable relationships during their formative years, leading to an intense worry that they will be rejected or left alone. This fear can manifest in controlling behaviors, manipulation, or superficial connections, as they attempt to maintain a sense of security and control over their relationships.

To address this fear, individuals can benefit from developing healthier attachment styles. Engaging in open communication, seeking reassurance in a constructive manner, and learning to trust others can help reduce the anxiety associated with perceived abandonment. Building genuine connections based on mutual respect and understanding can also mitigate this fear.

Fear of Vulnerability
The fear of vulnerability is a significant driving force behind narcissistic behavior. Many narcissists struggle to show their true selves, fearing that revealing their weaknesses will lead to judgment or rejection. This fear often prevents them from forming authentic relationships and contributes to a cycle of isolation and self-protection.

To confront this fear, individuals must practice vulnerability in safe environments. This could involve sharing personal thoughts and feelings with trusted friends or engaging in therapy to explore deeper emotional issues. Embracing vulnerability not only fosters deeper connections but also facilitates emotional healing, allowing individuals to step away from self-centeredness and toward empathy.

Fear of Being Unseen
A less commonly discussed fear that underlies narcissism is the fear of being unseen or unrecognized. In a world that often equates worth with visibility, narcissists may feel compelled to seek constant validation to ensure they are acknowledged. This fear can lead to attention-seeking behaviors, as they strive to assert their presence in various social circles.

Addressing this fear involves shifting the focus from external validation to internal acceptance. Techniques such as mindfulness and self-reflection can help individuals appreciate their intrinsic worth without relying on others for affirmation. Learning to celebrate personal achievements privately and finding fulfillment in meaningful activities can alleviate the need for excessive external recognition.

Conclusion
Identifying the core fears behind narcissism is a vital step toward healing. By understanding that narcissistic behavior often stems from fears of inadequacy, abandonment, vulnerability, and being unseen, individuals can begin to dismantle the defenses they have built. Emphasizing self-compassion and fostering genuine connections allows for a transformative journey from self-centeredness to self-awareness. Ultimately, recognizing these fears can lead to a more authentic, empathetic existence, paving the way for healthier relationships and personal growth.

Shifting from External Validation to Internal Validation
The journey from external validation to internal validation is a crucial step in overcoming narcissistic tendencies and fostering genuine self-worth. External validation refers to the approval, recognition, or affirmation sought from others, which can often manifest as a need for admiration, praise, or validation from peers, family, or social media. In contrast, internal

validation stems from within, allowing individuals to recognize their value independent of outside opinions. This shift is not only essential for personal growth but also for building healthier relationships and developing a more authentic sense of self.

Understanding the Need for External Validation

For many individuals, especially those with narcissistic traits, external validation can become a primary source of self-esteem. This dependency often develops during childhood, where praise and approval from caregivers may have been contingent on certain behaviors or achievements. As a result, individuals learn to gauge their self-worth based on external feedback, leading to a fragile self-esteem that fluctuates with the opinions of others. This validation-seeking behavior can create a cycle of anxiety, as individuals constantly strive for approval, fearing criticism or rejection.

Recognizing the Harmful Effects

The reliance on external validation can have detrimental effects on mental health and relationships. It can result in an unstable sense of self, where feelings of worth fluctuate dramatically based on the responses of others. This dependency can lead to feelings of shame and inadequacy when faced with criticism, fostering defensiveness or aggression in interpersonal interactions. Ultimately, the pursuit of external validation can hinder personal authenticity and create barriers to forming meaningful relationships, as individuals may present a curated version of themselves to gain approval.

Embracing Internal Validation

To shift from external to internal validation, individuals must begin to cultivate self-awareness and self-acceptance. This process involves recognizing and challenging the deeply ingrained beliefs that tie self-worth to external approval. Here are several steps that can facilitate this transition:

1. Self-Reflection: Engage in regular self-reflection to identify personal values, strengths, and achievements. Journaling can be a powerful tool to document thoughts and feelings, helping individuals connect with their intrinsic worth.

2. Acknowledge Achievements: Celebrate personal successes, no matter how small. By recognizing accomplishments without seeking others' approval, individuals can build a sense of pride and self-recognition.

3. Practice Self-Compassion: Developing self-compassion involves treating oneself with kindness during failures or setbacks. This practice encourages a more forgiving and understanding internal dialogue, reducing the need for external validation.

4. Set Personal Goals: Establish personal goals that align with individual values and aspirations, rather than those dictated by societal expectations or peer pressure. Focus on intrinsic motivations, which can foster a sense of fulfillment independent of external feedback.

5. Mindfulness Practices: Mindfulness techniques, such as meditation, can help cultivate present-moment awareness, allowing individuals to observe their thoughts and feelings without judgment. This practice can promote a deeper understanding of oneself, leading to greater internal validation.

6. Limit Social Comparison: Actively work to reduce comparisons with others, particularly on social media. Recognize that curated representations of life on platforms often do not reflect reality, and instead focus on personal growth and progress.

7. Seek Feedback Wisely: While constructive feedback can be beneficial, it's essential to approach it with a discerning mindset. Learn to differentiate between helpful critiques and opinions that may not align with personal values or growth.

Conclusion

Shifting from external validation to internal validation is a transformative process that can significantly enhance self-esteem and emotional well-being. By fostering a deeper connection with oneself, individuals can build resilience against the pressures of societal expectations and cultivate more authentic relationships. This journey not only leads to personal fulfillment but also paves the way for a more empathetic and compassionate way of engaging with others, ultimately contributing to a healthier, more balanced life.

Practicing Humility: Learning to Accept Imperfection

Humility is an essential quality that often stands in stark contrast to the traits associated with narcissism. While narcissism thrives on self-aggrandizement, superiority, and an inflated sense of self-importance, humility encourages a balanced perspective of oneself in relation to others and the world. This section delves into the importance of practicing humility and learning to accept imperfection as a key step towards healing from narcissistic tendencies.

Understanding Humility

At its core, humility is the recognition of and willingness to accept one's limitations and imperfections. It does not mean thinking less of oneself but rather thinking of oneself less.

Humble individuals acknowledge their strengths without exaggeration while being cognizant of their weaknesses. This balanced self-perception fosters a healthier relationship with oneself and others, promoting empathy, compassion, and connection.

The Role of Imperfection in Growth

Accepting imperfection is crucial for personal growth and emotional well-being. In a culture that often glorifies perfection, many individuals, particularly those struggling with narcissistic traits, may develop an unhealthy fear of failure and criticism. This fear can lead to defensive behaviors, avoidance, and self-sabotage. Embracing imperfection allows individuals to see mistakes and shortcomings as opportunities for learning rather than threats to their self-worth.

When individuals learn to accept that everyone has flaws and makes mistakes, they can cultivate a more forgiving attitude towards themselves and others. This shift in perspective fosters resilience, as it encourages a growth mindset—one that views challenges as chances to improve rather than insurmountable barriers.

Techniques to Foster Humility

1. Mindful Self-Reflection: Regular self-reflection through journaling or meditation can help cultivate humility. By taking time to reflect on one's actions, thoughts, and feelings, individuals can gain insight into their motivations and behaviors. This practice encourages a deeper understanding of one's imperfections, promoting acceptance and compassion.

2. Seeking Feedback: Actively seeking constructive feedback from others can enhance humility. It opens opportunities for personal growth by providing external perspectives on one's behavior and actions. Embracing feedback—even when it may be uncomfortable—can help dismantle the barriers of defensiveness that often accompany narcissistic traits.

3. Practicing Gratitude: Gratitude shifts the focus from self-centeredness to appreciation for others and the world around us. By recognizing and valuing the contributions of others, individuals can foster a sense of interconnectedness and humility. Keeping a gratitude journal can be an effective tool for this practice, encouraging reflection on the positive aspects of life and the people who enrich it.

4. Engaging in Community Service: Serving others can profoundly impact one's perspective. Volunteering or helping those in need helps individuals step outside of themselves, fostering empathy and a sense of purpose. This not only promotes humility but also reinforces the understanding that our worth is not solely defined by personal accomplishments.

5. Embracing Vulnerability: Allowing oneself to be vulnerable—whether by admitting mistakes, sharing fears, or asking for help—can be a powerful way to develop humility. Vulnerability fosters connection and authenticity, breaking down the barriers that narcissistic tendencies often erect in relationships.

Conclusion
Practicing humility and learning to accept imperfection is a transformative process that can significantly impact one's emotional health and interpersonal relationships. By embracing the inherent value of being human—complete with flaws and imperfections—individuals can cultivate a more authentic, empathetic, and fulfilling life. This journey towards humility not only aids personal growth but also fosters deeper connections with others, ultimately leading to a richer, more meaningful existence devoid of narcissistic tendencies.

Developing Gratitude: A Key to Healing Narcissistic Tendencies
Gratitude is often heralded as a transformative practice that can shift one's focus from self-centeredness to a broader appreciation of life and the people within it. For those struggling with narcissistic tendencies, cultivating gratitude can serve as a powerful antidote to the pervasive traits of entitlement, self-absorption, and the need for external validation.

Understanding the Role of Gratitude in Healing
At its core, gratitude involves recognizing the positive aspects of life and acknowledging the contributions of others, fostering a sense of connection and appreciation. This practice encourages individuals to look beyond themselves, breaking the cycle of self-referential thinking that often characterizes narcissism. By shifting attention from one's own needs and desires to the blessings and support received from others, individuals can begin to cultivate a more balanced perspective.

Research has shown that gratitude can increase feelings of well-being, enhance relationships, and promote emotional resilience. For individuals with narcissistic traits, these benefits can lead to a reduction in the defensive mechanisms that often arise from feelings of inadequacy or fear of rejection. Instead of operating from a place of perceived scarcity, gratitude fosters a mindset of abundance, where individuals can recognize the value and worth of others and themselves.

Practical Steps to Cultivate Gratitude

1. Gratitude Journaling: One effective way to develop gratitude is through journaling. Setting aside time each day to write down three to five things for which one is grateful can help shift focus from negative thought patterns. This practice encourages mindfulness and reflection, allowing individuals to acknowledge both small and significant blessings in their lives. Over time, this exercise can help rewire the brain to recognize positivity more readily.

2. Expressing Appreciation: Another powerful method is to actively express gratitude towards others. This can be as simple as sending a thank-you note, verbally acknowledging someone's contribution, or performing acts of kindness. By recognizing and appreciating others, individuals can strengthen their relationships, fostering a sense of connection that counteracts the isolating tendencies of narcissism.

3. Mindfulness and Presence: Integrating mindfulness practices can enhance gratitude. Mindfulness encourages individuals to be present in the moment, which can lead to a deeper appreciation of life's simple pleasures. Whether it's savoring a meal, enjoying nature, or being fully engaged in conversations, mindfulness can help individuals develop a sense of gratitude for everyday experiences.

4. Reframing Negative Thoughts: Developing gratitude also involves reframing negative thoughts and experiences. Instead of viewing challenges solely through a lens of self-pity or frustration, individuals can look for lessons or growth opportunities. This shift in perspective fosters resilience and can diminish the need for external validation, as individuals learn to find value in their experiences.

5. Participating in Community Service: Engaging in acts of service can significantly enhance feelings of gratitude. Volunteering for community projects or helping those in need allows individuals to step outside themselves and recognize the impact they can have on others' lives. This not only fosters a sense of purpose but also reinforces the understanding that life is about contributing to the well-being of others.

Long-Term Benefits of Gratitude in Healing

Incorporating gratitude into daily life is not a quick fix but rather a journey toward healing. For those with narcissistic tendencies, developing gratitude can lead to profound shifts in self-perception and relational dynamics. Over time, individuals may find themselves less reliant on external validation and more content with their intrinsic worth.

By embracing gratitude, individuals can cultivate empathy, foster deeper connections, and ultimately lead a more fulfilling and balanced life. This shift not only benefits the individual but also enriches the lives of those around them, creating a positive ripple effect that can transform relationships and communities.

Building Healthy Self-Esteem Without Narcissism

Self-esteem is a crucial aspect of mental and emotional well-being. It serves as the foundation for how we perceive ourselves and our interactions with the world. However, distinguishing between healthy self-esteem and narcissism can be challenging. While both involve self-regard, narcissism is characterized by an inflated sense of self-importance, a need for excessive admiration, and a lack of empathy for others. Building healthy self-esteem involves cultivating self-worth that is genuine, sustainable, and rooted in self-acceptance rather than external validation.

Understanding Healthy Self-Esteem

Healthy self-esteem means having a realistic view of oneself, recognizing both strengths and weaknesses. It allows individuals to appreciate their worth without diminishing others. People with healthy self-esteem are confident but not arrogant; they embrace humility while acknowledging their achievements. This balanced perspective fosters resilience, enabling one to cope with challenges and setbacks constructively.

Shifting Focus from External Validation

One of the hallmarks of narcissistic tendencies is an excessive reliance on external validation—seeking praise, admiration, and approval from others. To build healthy self-esteem, it is essential to shift focus inward. This means recognizing personal strengths and achievements without needing constant affirmation from others. A practical approach is to keep a daily journal where you document accomplishments, no matter how small, and reflect on personal values and qualities that define your self-worth.

Practicing Self-Compassion

Self-compassion is a critical component of healthy self-esteem. It involves treating oneself with kindness and understanding during times of failure or difficulty rather than resorting to self-criticism. When setbacks occur, individuals can practice self-compassion by acknowledging their feelings, recognizing that imperfection is a part of being human, and committing to learn from experiences. Techniques such as mindfulness meditation can assist in cultivating self-compassion, allowing individuals to approach their thoughts and feelings with greater awareness and acceptance.

Embracing Imperfections

Accepting imperfections is vital in building healthy self-esteem. Narcissism often stems from a fear of inadequacy, leading individuals to create a facade of perfectionism. In contrast, embracing imperfections fosters authenticity. Accepting that everyone has flaws and makes mistakes can alleviate the pressure to perform flawlessly, encouraging a more realistic self-image. Engaging in activities that challenge comfort zones, such as trying new hobbies or skills, can reinforce the idea that growth and learning come from embracing vulnerability.

Cultivating Gratitude
Gratitude plays an essential role in nurturing healthy self-esteem. By regularly reflecting on what you are grateful for, you shift focus away from self-centeredness and toward appreciation of life's positive aspects. This practice can help mitigate feelings of entitlement and comparison, which often fuel narcissistic thoughts. A gratitude journal can be an effective tool, where individuals list three things they appreciate about themselves, their lives, or others each day.

Setting Realistic Goals
Goal-setting is another significant aspect of developing healthy self-esteem. Setting realistic, achievable goals encourages a sense of accomplishment and reinforces self-worth. It is important to focus on intrinsic goals—those that are fulfilling and contribute to personal development—rather than extrinsic goals tied to external validation. Celebrating small victories along the way can help maintain motivation and a positive self-image.

Seeking Support and Connection
Building healthy self-esteem is often enhanced through supportive relationships. Engaging with friends, family, or support groups can provide encouragement and positive reinforcement. Healthy relationships cultivate a sense of belonging and foster mutual respect, reducing the need for excessive self-promotion or validation.

In conclusion, building healthy self-esteem without falling into narcissism involves a multi-faceted approach. By fostering self-compassion, embracing imperfections, cultivating gratitude, and engaging in supportive relationships, individuals can create a robust sense of self-worth that is both authentic and sustainable. This journey toward self-acceptance not only enhances personal well-being but also enriches relationships with others, fostering deeper connections based on empathy and mutual respect.

Chapter 6

Healing from Narcissistic Traits

Acknowledging the Need for Change

Acknowledging the need for change is a fundamental first step in the journey toward healing from narcissistic traits. This process is often challenging, as it requires a deep level of self-reflection, vulnerability, and the willingness to confront uncomfortable truths about oneself. For individuals who exhibit narcissistic behaviors, recognizing the need for change can be particularly daunting due to the inherent defensiveness and self-justification that often accompany such traits. However, this acknowledgment is crucial not only for personal growth but also for creating healthier relationships and a more fulfilling life.

The Challenge of Self-Recognition

Self-awareness is the cornerstone of personal transformation. Many individuals with narcissistic tendencies possess a distorted self-image that leads them to overestimate their capabilities and value. This inflated self-perception can create a blind spot for recognizing the negative impact of their behaviors on themselves and those around them. To begin the journey of change, individuals must confront their denial and defensiveness, which often serve as barriers to understanding their actions and their consequences.

Practicing self-reflection is essential in this regard. Engaging in honest introspection allows individuals to evaluate their patterns of behavior, emotional responses, and the repercussions those have on their relationships. Keeping a journal can be a powerful tool in this endeavor. Writing down feelings, thoughts, and experiences can help clarify one's motivations and behaviors, providing insights that may not be immediately visible in the hustle and bustle of daily life.

Understanding the Motivation for Change

Acknowledging the need for change is not merely about recognizing faults; it is also about understanding the underlying motivations for wanting to change. Many individuals may be driven by external pressures, such as the desire for better relationships or professional success. However, sustainable change often requires an internal motivation—a genuine desire to grow, heal, and cultivate healthier interactions with oneself and others.

Self-compassion plays a critical role in this process. Instead of harsh self-criticism, individuals should approach themselves with kindness and understanding. Recognizing that everyone has flaws and that growth is a lifelong journey can help ease the fear associated with acknowledging personal shortcomings. Embracing the idea that making mistakes is part of being human can foster a more accepting mindset, making it easier to confront and address narcissistic tendencies.

The Role of Accountability
Accountability is an essential component of acknowledging the need for change. This means taking responsibility for one's actions and their impact on others. Rather than deflecting blame or minimizing the consequences of narcissistic behavior, individuals must commit to owning their actions. This may involve having difficult conversations with those affected by their behavior, sincerely apologizing, and expressing a genuine desire to change.

Establishing a support system is also crucial for fostering accountability. Surrounding oneself with trustworthy friends, family members, or a therapist can provide external perspectives and encouragement during the change process. They can help hold individuals accountable, offer constructive feedback, and remind them of their commitment to personal growth when challenges arise.

Embracing Vulnerability as a Strength
Finally, acknowledging the need for change requires embracing vulnerability. For many, vulnerability is perceived as a weakness, especially for those with narcissistic traits, who often fear exposure and rejection. However, true strength lies in the ability to be open and honest about one's struggles and desires for growth. Embracing vulnerability allows individuals to connect more deeply with others, foster empathy, and ultimately build more authentic relationships.

In conclusion, acknowledging the need for change is a vital step on the path to overcoming narcissistic tendencies. Through self-reflection, understanding motivations, embracing accountability, and recognizing the power of vulnerability, individuals can embark on a transformative journey that not only enhances their self-awareness but also enriches their relationships and overall quality of life.

The Importance of Vulnerability in Growth
Vulnerability is often perceived as a weakness in a society that prizes strength, control, and self-sufficiency, particularly for individuals displaying narcissistic traits. However, true personal growth and healing from narcissistic tendencies hinge on embracing vulnerability as a powerful, transformative tool. Understanding and accepting vulnerability can lead to deeper self-awareness, authentic relationships, and a profound shift in how one interacts with the

world.

Understanding Vulnerability

At its core, vulnerability is the willingness to expose one's true self, including feelings, fears, and imperfections. It requires stepping away from the façade of invulnerability that narcissistic individuals often maintain to protect themselves from perceived threats to their self-esteem. This façade can manifest as arrogance, self-centeredness, or a relentless need for admiration. However, the reality is that true strength comes from acknowledging one's flaws and uncertainties.

By embracing vulnerability, individuals can confront the underlying insecurities that drive narcissistic behavior. For example, many narcissists harbor a deep fear of inadequacy or rejection. Acknowledging these fears can lead to a healthier understanding of oneself and facilitate the journey toward personal growth.

Vulnerability as a Pathway to Connection

In relationships, vulnerability is essential for building trust and intimacy. Narcissistic traits often lead to superficial connections, where the focus is on self-promotion rather than genuine engagement with others. By allowing oneself to be vulnerable, individuals can break down barriers that prevent authentic relationships from forming. This process involves sharing personal experiences, admitting mistakes, and expressing emotions honestly.

Research by Brené Brown, a prominent researcher on vulnerability, shows that vulnerability fosters empathy and connection. When individuals share their struggles, others can relate and respond with compassion, creating a supportive environment conducive to growth. For those healing from narcissistic behaviors, this shift from self-centered interactions to empathetic connections can be transformative.

The Role of Vulnerability in Self-Reflection

Self-reflection is a critical component of personal growth, and vulnerability enhances this process. Engaging in self-reflection requires one to confront uncomfortable truths about oneself, including narcissistic traits. This process can be daunting, as it necessitates facing criticism and acknowledging past mistakes. However, vulnerability allows individuals to approach self-reflection with openness rather than defensiveness.

By being vulnerable, individuals can ask themselves probing questions: What drives my need for admiration? How do my actions affect those around me? These reflections can lead to insights that are crucial for healing. Acknowledging one's shortcomings is not an admission of failure but rather a courageous step toward self-improvement.

Cultivating a Growth Mindset Through Vulnerability
Embracing vulnerability is integral to developing a growth mindset—the belief that abilities and intelligence can be developed with effort and learning. This mindset contrasts sharply with a fixed mindset that often accompanies narcissism, where individuals view their worth as static and contingent on external validation.

When individuals allow themselves to be vulnerable, they open the door to learning from mistakes and accepting constructive criticism. This shift enables them to see challenges as opportunities for growth rather than threats to their self-worth. For instance, someone who previously reacted defensively to feedback can learn to view it as a valuable tool for improvement when they embrace vulnerability.

Conclusion
In conclusion, vulnerability is not a weakness; it is a vital strength that propels individuals toward personal growth and healthier relationships. For those struggling with narcissistic traits, embracing vulnerability can facilitate deeper self-awareness, foster authentic connections, and cultivate a growth mindset. By acknowledging their fears and imperfections, individuals can embark on a transformative journey that leads to healing and a more fulfilling life. Embracing vulnerability may be challenging, but it is a necessary step toward living an authentic, empathetic, and connected life.

Learning to Apologize and Repair
Apologizing is a crucial component of emotional intelligence and relationship maintenance. It serves not only as a means of expressing remorse but also as a pathway to healing and reconciliation. For individuals struggling with narcissistic traits, the act of apologizing can be particularly challenging. This difficulty often stems from a heightened sensitivity to perceived criticism, a fear of vulnerability, and a tendency to defend oneself rather than acknowledge wrongdoing. However, learning how to apologize sincerely and effectively is a vital step in the journey toward healing and building healthier relationships.

The Importance of a Genuine Apology
A genuine apology goes beyond merely saying "I'm sorry." It involves acknowledging the specific behavior that caused harm, expressing understanding of how that behavior affected the other person, and taking responsibility for it. This process is not only about making the wronged party feel better; it is also an opportunity for the apologizer to demonstrate personal growth and emotional maturity.

1. Acknowledgment: The first step in crafting a genuine apology is recognizing the impact of one's actions. This requires introspection and a willingness to step outside one's own perspective. Acknowledging the hurt caused by one's behavior is essential to making the other person feel seen and valued.

2. Empathy: Following acknowledgment, it is critical to express empathy. This means articulating how the other person may have felt as a result of the behavior. Words like, "I can see how my actions made you feel hurt" show that you are not only aware of the offense but also sensitive to the emotional aftermath it caused.

3. Responsibility: Taking full responsibility for one's actions is often the most challenging aspect of an apology, especially for individuals with narcissistic tendencies. It requires setting aside the instinct to deflect blame or rationalize behavior. Accepting responsibility means saying, "I was wrong, and I take full accountability for it."

4. Repair Efforts: An effective apology includes a commitment to making amends and changing future behavior. This might involve specific actions, such as making a promise to communicate better or actively working to avoid repeating the same mistakes. By outlining a plan for change, you demonstrate a genuine desire to repair the relationship.

5. Timing and Sincerity: Timing is crucial when it comes to apologies. It's important to choose a moment when emotions have settled and genuine communication can occur. Additionally, sincerity must be at the forefront of your apology; it cannot be merely a tactical move to ease discomfort or manipulate the situation.

Overcoming Barriers to Apologizing

For those inclined toward narcissism, several barriers can hinder the apology process:

- Fear of Vulnerability: Apologizing requires exposing oneself to potential rejection or further criticism, which can be intimidating. Practicing vulnerability in safe environments can help individuals become more comfortable with the process.

- Defensiveness: The instinct to become defensive when confronted can impede the ability to apologize. Engaging in self-reflection and mindfulness can help in recognizing these defensive reactions and choosing to respond differently.

- Shame and Guilt: Feelings of shame can lead to avoidance of accountability. Learning to reframe these feelings as opportunities for growth rather than as personal failures can motivate the individual to apologize rather than withdraw.

The Path to Healing
Once an apology is made, the next step is to engage in the repair process. This involves not just the words spoken but also the actions that follow. Genuine, consistent efforts to rebuild trust and demonstrate change can help mend relationships and foster deeper connections.

Ultimately, learning to apologize and repair relationships is a journey that requires courage, humility, and a commitment to personal growth. By embracing this process, individuals can cultivate healthier interactions and foster empathy, paving the way for more fulfilling connections with others.

Forgiving Yourself: Letting Go of Past Mistakes
Forgiving oneself is a crucial aspect of healing from narcissistic traits and fostering emotional growth. Many individuals grappling with narcissism often harbor deep-seated guilt and shame associated with their past behaviors. These emotions can create a cycle of self-criticism and defensiveness, further entrenching narcissistic patterns. Understanding the process of self-forgiveness can be a transformative step towards personal accountability and emotional well-being.

Understanding Self-Forgiveness
Self-forgiveness is not merely about absolving oneself of guilt; it is a profound act of kindness towards oneself. It involves acknowledging past mistakes, accepting the impact of those actions on oneself and others, and ultimately making peace with the past. This process is essential for breaking the cycle of narcissism, as it fosters a healthier self-image grounded in compassion rather than self-loathing.

The Importance of Acknowledgment
The first step toward self-forgiveness involves recognizing and acknowledging the mistakes made. This requires an honest reflection on actions and behaviors that may have caused harm to oneself or others. For those struggling with narcissistic tendencies, this acknowledgment can be particularly challenging, as it may trigger feelings of shame and vulnerability. However, facing these feelings head-on is essential for growth. Journaling can be a powerful tool in this phase, allowing individuals to articulate their thoughts and emotions, thus clarifying their experiences.

Accepting Responsibility
Once past actions have been acknowledged, the next step is accepting responsibility. This means recognizing that while mistakes were made, they do not define one's entire identity.

Accepting responsibility allows individuals to learn from their errors and understand the consequences of their actions. It is critical to approach this step with self-compassion; rather than berating oneself, it's important to view these experiences as opportunities for growth. This shift in perspective can help mitigate feelings of shame.

The Role of Empathy

Cultivating empathy is a significant part of the self-forgiveness process. Understanding how one's actions affected others can deepen our emotional awareness and encourage a more compassionate view of ourselves. Engaging in perspective-taking—considering how others might feel as a result of our actions—can help bridge the gap between self-criticism and self-compassion. This empathetic approach not only helps in the pursuit of self-forgiveness but also strengthens interpersonal relationships, as it fosters a greater understanding of others' experiences.

Making Amends

Making amends can be a powerful step toward self-forgiveness. This doesn't necessarily mean seeking forgiveness from those we've hurt; rather, it can involve taking concrete steps to rectify past wrongs or to change future behavior. It might include reaching out to apologize, engaging in acts of kindness, or simply committing to personal growth. Such actions can reinforce the concept that one is capable of change, which is vital for healing from narcissistic tendencies.

Letting Go and Moving Forward

Finally, letting go of the past is essential for self-forgiveness. This requires a conscious decision to release the grip of past mistakes and to embrace the possibility of change. Techniques such as mindfulness and meditation can be beneficial in this regard, as they promote present-moment awareness and help individuals detach from negative thought patterns associated with guilt and shame.

In conclusion, forgiving yourself is a vital step in the journey of healing from narcissism. By acknowledging mistakes, accepting responsibility, cultivating empathy, making amends, and ultimately letting go, individuals can break free from the chains of their past. This process not only leads to personal growth but also paves the way for healthier, more authentic relationships. Embracing self-forgiveness allows for a life characterized by compassion, integrity, and the capacity for genuine connection, marking a significant departure from narcissistic tendencies.

Rebuilding Trust in Relationships

Trust is the cornerstone of any healthy relationship, acting as a vital glue that holds connections together. When narcissistic behaviors have contributed to a breakdown of trust—whether through manipulation, dishonesty, or emotional neglect—rebuilding that trust becomes a crucial, albeit challenging, task. The journey to restore trust requires introspection, accountability, and consistent effort.

Acknowledging Past Actions

The first step in rebuilding trust is acknowledging the behaviors that led to its erosion. This involves a deep and honest self-reflection regarding past actions that may have caused pain to others. Individuals must confront their narcissistic tendencies, such as a lack of empathy, defensiveness, or a propensity to dismiss the feelings of others. By recognizing and articulating these behaviors, one can begin the process of accountability, which is essential for healing.

Open Communication

Rebuilding trust necessitates open and transparent communication. Initiating conversations about past hurts and misunderstandings allows both parties to voice their feelings and experiences. This dialogue should be approached with humility and a willingness to listen without becoming defensive. It is vital to validate the feelings of those who were affected by narcissistic behaviors, acknowledging their pain and demonstrating a genuine desire to understand their perspective.

Consistent Actions

Words must be matched with actions. To regain trust, it is crucial to demonstrate reliability and consistency over time. This means following through on promises, being present, and showing that you value the relationship. Small gestures can make a significant difference—whether it's being punctual, actively listening during conversations, or offering support in times of need. Consistency helps to rebuild the sense of security that may have been lost.

Setting Healthy Boundaries

Part of restoring trust involves establishing healthy boundaries. Understanding and respecting the limits of others is essential, especially if past narcissistic tendencies led to boundary violations. Open discussions about boundaries should be prioritized, allowing both individuals to express their needs and comfort levels. This mutual respect fosters a safe environment where trust can gradually be rebuilt.

Practicing Vulnerability

Vulnerability plays a key role in rebuilding trust. Sharing one's fears, insecurities, and experiences of remorse can help to humanize the individual who has engaged in narcissistic behaviors. By allowing oneself to be vulnerable, it not only shows the other person that you are committed to change but also opens the door for them to share their feelings and experiences. This exchange fosters deeper emotional connections and understanding.

Forgiveness and Healing
Trust rebuilding also involves the concept of forgiveness, both for the individual who has caused harm and for the one who has been hurt. Forgiveness does not mean condoning past behaviors but rather letting go of the hold that those experiences have on future interactions. Healing requires time and patience, and it is essential to recognize that trust is rebuilt incrementally, not instantaneously.

Seeking Professional Help
In some cases, the assistance of a therapist or counselor can be invaluable. Professional guidance can provide tools for effective communication, conflict resolution, and emotional healing. Therapy can create a safe space for both individuals to explore their feelings, address underlying issues, and learn healthier ways to interact.

Conclusion
Rebuilding trust in relationships affected by narcissistic behavior is a challenging yet rewarding endeavor. It requires a commitment to self-improvement, open communication, and a willingness to embrace vulnerability. By taking consistent and meaningful steps towards accountability and empathy, individuals can restore trust and foster healthier, more authentic connections. While the journey may be fraught with difficulties, it ultimately leads to stronger, more resilient relationships built on mutual respect and understanding.

Chapter 7

Coping with Narcissistic Injuries

Understanding Narcissistic Injuries

Narcissistic injuries refer to the emotional wounds experienced by individuals with narcissistic traits when their self-esteem or self-image is threatened. These injuries can arise from various triggers, including criticism, rejection, failure, or perceived slights—essentially any situation that challenges their inflated sense of self-worth. Understanding these injuries is crucial in addressing the underlying issues of narcissism and fostering healthier emotional responses.

The Nature of Narcissistic Injuries

At the core of narcissistic injuries lies a fragile self-esteem masked by grandiosity. Individuals with narcissistic tendencies often project an image of superiority and invulnerability. However, beneath this facade is a deep-seated need for validation and affirmation. When they encounter situations that contradict this self-image, they experience what can be described as a narcissistic injury. This reaction is akin to a psychological wound, eliciting intense emotions such as shame, humiliation, anger, or despair.

For example, a narcissistic individual may react disproportionately to constructive criticism, perceiving it not merely as feedback but as a direct attack on their identity. The injury can trigger defensive behaviors, such as anger or withdrawal, as a means to protect their vulnerable self-esteem. Understanding this dynamic is vital for both the individual experiencing these injuries and those interacting with them.

Triggers of Narcissistic Injuries

Several common triggers can lead to narcissistic injuries:

1. Criticism and Rejection: Feedback that challenges their self-image or performance can be perceived as a threat. This may include job performance reviews, personal critiques, or even casual remarks that highlight their flaws.

2. Failure: Situations where they do not achieve expected outcomes can evoke feelings of inadequacy. This could range from failing to meet personal goals to experiencing setbacks in professional endeavors.

3. Comparison: Narcissistic individuals often compare themselves to others to gauge their self-worth. Seeing someone else succeed or receive recognition can lead to feelings of envy and trigger a sense of inadequacy.

4. Loss of Control: Situations where they feel they lack power—whether in relationships or professional settings—can provoke anxiety and lead to reactive behaviors aimed at regaining a sense of superiority.

5. Perceived Indifference: A lack of acknowledgment or attention from others can also trigger narcissistic injuries, as these individuals often rely on external validation to feel valued.

The Impact of Narcissistic Injuries on Behavior
When narcissistic injuries occur, the response can manifest in various maladaptive behaviors:

- **Defensiveness:** Rather than reflecting on the feedback or situation, individuals may become defensive, dismissing criticism or attacking the source of the perceived injury.

- **Blame-Shifting:** They may deflect responsibility for failures or mistakes, attributing them to external circumstances or others to protect their self-image.

- **Withdrawal:** In some cases, narcissistic individuals may retreat from social interactions, feeling too vulnerable to engage with others.

- **Aggression:** Narcissistic injuries can lead to aggressive outbursts, where the individual lashes out verbally or emotionally against those they perceive as threats.

Healing from Narcissistic Injuries
Understanding and addressing narcissistic injuries is essential for personal growth. It requires cultivating emotional resilience and developing healthier coping mechanisms. Here are some steps individuals can take:

1. Self-Reflection: Engaging in honest self-reflection can help individuals recognize and understand their emotional responses to perceived threats.

2. Seeking Feedback: Learning to accept constructive criticism without personalizing it can foster growth and reduce the likelihood of defensive reactions.

3. Therapeutic Support: Working with a therapist specializing in narcissistic traits can provide valuable insights and strategies for managing emotional wounds.

4. Developing Empathy: Fostering empathy for others can shift focus away from the self and reduce the intensity of narcissistic injuries.

By acknowledging the roots of narcissistic injuries and actively working towards healing, individuals can transform their emotional landscape, leading to healthier relationships and a more authentic sense of self.

Identifying Triggers and Learning to Respond Differently

Understanding and managing narcissistic tendencies requires a keen awareness of personal triggers—events, interactions, or feelings that provoke defensive or self-centered reactions. Identifying these triggers is a crucial step in fostering self-awareness and initiating change. This process not only aids in personal growth but also enhances relationships, as it encourages healthier responses to stressors.

Understanding Triggers

Triggers can manifest in various forms, often rooted in past experiences or insecurities. Common triggers for individuals with narcissistic traits include criticism, rejection, perceived inadequacy, and comparison to others. These situations can evoke intense emotional responses such as anger, shame, or anxiety, often leading to defensive mechanisms like denial, blame-shifting, or excessive self-promotion.

For instance, receiving constructive feedback may trigger feelings of inadequacy, provoking a defensive attack on the critic instead of fostering growth. Similarly, social situations that highlight one's insecurities, such as gatherings where achievements are discussed, can trigger feelings of envy or the need for validation. Recognizing these patterns is essential for breaking the cycle of reactive behavior.

Self-Reflection Practices

To identify personal triggers, self-reflection is vital. Journaling is an effective tool for this purpose. By documenting daily experiences and emotional reactions, individuals can begin to identify recurring themes and situations that elicit strong responses. Questions to consider include:

- What situations make me feel defensive or irritable?
- How do I typically react in these moments?
- Are there specific words or actions from others that trigger my emotional responses?

Engaging in mindfulness practices can also enhance self-awareness. Mindfulness encourages individuals to stay present and observe their thoughts and feelings without judgment. This practice can help in recognizing when a trigger is activated and create space for thoughtful responses rather than knee-jerk reactions.

Learning to Respond Differently

Once triggers are identified, the next step is to develop healthier responses. This requires a shift in mindset, moving from a reactive to a proactive approach. Here are some strategies to facilitate this change:

1. Pause and Breathe: When a trigger is activated, it's helpful to take a moment to breathe deeply and assess the situation. This pause can prevent an immediate, emotional response and open the door for thoughtful consideration.

2. Reframe the Narrative: Instead of viewing criticism or rejection as a personal attack, reframe it as an opportunity for growth. This mental shift can help mitigate feelings of shame and reduce defensiveness.

3. Practice Empathy: When faced with a trigger, consider the perspectives of others involved. Asking questions like, "What might they be feeling?" or "What is their intention?" can foster compassion and reduce feelings of personal attack.

4. Develop Problem-Solving Skills: Instead of reacting defensively, approach the trigger as a problem to be solved. For example, if a colleague's feedback triggers defensiveness, consider how that feedback can be used constructively to enhance one's skills.

5. Seek Support: Engaging with a therapist or support group can provide valuable insights and coping strategies. Professional guidance can help navigate the complexities of emotional triggers and reactions.

Moving Forward

Identifying triggers and learning to respond differently is a continuous process that requires patience and commitment. As individuals develop greater awareness of their emotional responses, they can cultivate healthier interactions and relationships. This journey not only fosters personal growth but also promotes emotional resilience, paving the way for a more balanced, fulfilling life free from the constraints of narcissistic behavior. By embracing vulnerability and accountability, individuals can transform their responses and, ultimately, their relationships with themselves and others.

Managing Criticism and Rejection: Tools for Handling Ego Bruises

Criticism and rejection are inherent aspects of life, yet they can be particularly challenging for individuals grappling with narcissistic tendencies. The emotional wounds caused by these experiences can trigger defensive reactions and exacerbate narcissistic behaviors. Understanding how to manage these feelings is crucial for personal growth and emotional resilience. Here, we explore effective tools and strategies to handle the bruises to one's ego that often accompany criticism and rejection.

1. Understanding the Emotional Response

The first step in managing criticism and rejection is recognizing the emotional responses they provoke. Individuals with narcissistic traits may experience intense feelings of shame, anger, or humiliation when faced with negative feedback. These feelings can lead to defensiveness, withdrawal, or aggressive retaliation. Acknowledging these emotions without judgment allows for a healthier processing of the experience. Journaling can be a beneficial tool for this, as it provides a safe space to explore feelings without immediate repercussions.

2. Cultivating Emotional Resilience

Building emotional resilience is vital in managing ego bruises. Emotional resilience refers to the ability to bounce back from setbacks and maintain a positive outlook in the face of adversity. Techniques to cultivate resilience include:

- **Mindfulness Practices:** Engaging in mindfulness meditation can help individuals stay grounded. By focusing on the present moment, one can observe their thoughts and feelings about criticism without becoming overwhelmed by them. This practice fosters a non-judgmental awareness that can diminish the sting of negative feedback.

- **Reframing Negative Thoughts:** Cognitive reframing involves changing the way you interpret a situation. Instead of viewing criticism as a personal attack, consider it an opportunity for growth. Ask yourself what constructive lessons can be learned from the feedback and how it can contribute to personal development.

3. Developing a Healthy Perspective on Criticism

Understanding that criticism is a natural part of life is essential. It is not always an indictment of one's character; often, it reflects the opinions or expectations of others. Adopting a growth mindset can facilitate a healthier relationship with criticism. This mindset emphasizes that abilities and intelligence can be developed through effort, learning, and perseverance.

4. Practicing Self-Compassion

Self-compassion plays a crucial role in managing the emotional fallout from criticism and rejection. Instead of harshly criticizing oneself after a setback, practice kindness towards oneself. This can involve:

- **Self-Talk:** Replace negative self-talk with compassionate affirmations. Remind yourself that everyone makes mistakes and faces criticism, and that such experiences do not define your worth.

- **Recognizing Common Humanity:** Understand that feeling hurt by criticism is a universal experience. This realization can diminish feelings of isolation and shame, fostering a sense of connection with others.

5. Implementing Constructive Responses

When faced with criticism, how one responds can significantly influence emotional well-being. Instead of reacting defensively, consider these proactive responses:

- **Active Listening:** When receiving feedback, focus on truly understanding the other person's perspective. Ask clarifying questions to ensure comprehension and demonstrate openness. This can help diffuse tensions and facilitate a more constructive dialogue.

- **Taking Time to Reflect:** If criticism feels overwhelming in the moment, allow yourself time to process before responding. This pause can prevent knee-jerk reactions and enable a more thoughtful reply.

6. Building a Supportive Network

Lastly, surrounding yourself with supportive individuals can buffer the negative effects of criticism and rejection. Seek out friends, family, or mentors who provide constructive feedback and encouragement. Their perspectives can offer a more balanced view of personal strengths and areas for improvement, making it easier to accept criticism without feeling diminished.

In conclusion, managing criticism and rejection requires a multifaceted approach that includes emotional awareness, resilience-building strategies, self-compassion, constructive responses, and a supportive network. By developing these tools, individuals can transform ego bruises into opportunities for growth, ultimately leading to healthier self-perceptions and improved relationships.

Building Emotional Resilience and Coping Skills

Building emotional resilience is essential for anyone seeking to manage and overcome narcissistic tendencies. Emotional resilience refers to the ability to adapt to stressful situations, recover from setbacks, and maintain a positive outlook despite adversity. For individuals struggling with narcissism, developing this resilience is crucial, as it allows them to navigate the emotional landscape of their lives with greater stability and awareness.

Understanding Emotional Resilience
Emotional resilience involves several key components: self-awareness, emotional regulation, social support, and adaptive coping strategies. While narcissistic traits may initially create a façade of invulnerability, they often mask underlying insecurities and emotional fragility. By fostering resilience, individuals can learn to confront these vulnerabilities rather than avoid them, leading to healthier emotional responses.

Self-Awareness
The foundation of emotional resilience is self-awareness. This involves recognizing one's emotions, triggers, and patterns of thought and behavior. Mindfulness practices, such as meditation or journaling, can help individuals gain insight into their emotional states. By reflecting on emotional responses to situations—especially those that provoke narcissistic reactions, such as criticism or perceived slights—individuals can begin to understand the root causes of their feelings. This awareness is the first step in developing healthier coping mechanisms.

Emotional Regulation
Emotional regulation is another critical aspect of resilience. It involves managing one's emotional responses to situations in a constructive manner. Techniques such as deep breathing, progressive muscle relaxation, or visualization can help individuals calm themselves during moments of distress. Additionally, practicing cognitive reframing—changing the way one interprets a situation—can reduce emotional reactivity. For example, instead of viewing criticism as a personal attack, one can reframe it as an opportunity for growth.

Building Social Support
A robust support network is essential for emotional resilience. Individuals struggling with narcissistic tendencies may find it challenging to maintain authentic relationships due to their self-centered behaviors. However, cultivating genuine connections with others can provide much-needed emotional support. Engaging with friends, family, or support groups can offer a space to express feelings, share experiences, and receive encouragement. It's important to seek relationships that are based on mutual respect and empathy, as these can help counteract the

isolating effects of narcissism.

Adaptive Coping Strategies
Developing adaptive coping strategies is crucial for managing emotional challenges. These strategies can range from problem-solving techniques to seeking professional help. Here are some effective approaches:

1. Problem-Solving: When faced with a challenge, break it down into manageable steps. Focus on actionable solutions rather than dwelling on negative emotions or blaming others.

2. Healthy Distraction: Engage in activities that promote joy and fulfillment, such as hobbies, exercise, or creative pursuits. This can provide a mental break and help alleviate stress.

3. Self-Compassion: Practice self-kindness during difficult times. Acknowledge that everyone makes mistakes and experiences setbacks, and treat yourself with the same compassion you would offer a friend.

4. Seeking Professional Help: Therapy can be an invaluable resource for building emotional resilience. A therapist can provide guidance, support, and tools to navigate emotional challenges, helping individuals develop healthier coping mechanisms.

5. Gratitude Practices: Cultivating gratitude can shift focus away from negative thoughts and enhance emotional well-being. Regularly reflecting on what one is thankful for can foster a more positive outlook on life.

Conclusion
Building emotional resilience and coping skills is a transformative process that empowers individuals to confront their narcissistic tendencies. Through self-awareness, emotional regulation, social support, and adaptive coping strategies, individuals can learn to navigate their emotional experiences with greater ease and stability. This journey not only promotes personal growth but also enhances relationships with others, paving the way for a more fulfilling and empathetic life.

Moving from Reactivity to Emotional Stability
The journey from reactivity to emotional stability is a critical aspect of personal growth, especially for individuals grappling with narcissistic tendencies. Reactivity is characterized by impulsive responses to emotional triggers, often leading to conflicts and misunderstandings in relationships. In contrast, emotional stability allows for measured, thoughtful responses that

foster healthier interactions and enhance overall well-being.

Understanding Reactivity

Reactivity often stems from unresolved emotional wounds or perceived threats to one's self-image. For individuals with narcissistic traits, this may manifest as defensiveness, anger, or withdrawal when faced with criticism or rejection. Such reactions are instinctual, designed to protect the ego but ultimately damaging to relationships and personal growth. Recognizing the triggers that lead to reactive behaviors is the first step toward cultivating emotional stability.

Identifying Triggers

The process of identifying triggers involves self-reflection and mindfulness. Keeping a journal can be a helpful tool in this regard. By documenting instances when reactivity occurs, individuals can begin to see patterns—specific situations, words, or behaviors that provoke strong emotional responses. This awareness helps create a mental map of potential pitfalls, allowing for proactive strategies to manage reactions before they escalate.

Developing Emotional Awareness

Emotional awareness is the foundation of emotional stability. It involves tuning into one's feelings and understanding their roots. This process can be enhanced through mindfulness practices such as meditation or deep-breathing exercises, which encourage individuals to pause and observe their emotions without judgment. By creating space between the trigger and the response, individuals can choose how to react, rather than defaulting to instinctual, defensive behaviors.

Practicing Emotional Regulation

Once awareness of triggers is established, the next step is developing emotional regulation skills. Techniques such as cognitive restructuring can be invaluable. This practice involves challenging negative thought patterns and replacing them with more balanced, constructive thoughts. For instance, instead of thinking, "I can't believe they criticized me; they must not respect me," one might reframe this to, "Their feedback is an opportunity for growth, and it doesn't define my worth."

Another useful tool is the practice of grounding techniques, which help individuals anchor themselves in the present moment. Simple exercises, such as focusing on the sensation of feet on the ground or paying attention to breathing, can help reduce the intensity of emotional responses and promote a sense of calm.

Building Resilience

Creating emotional stability also requires building resilience—an essential trait that enables individuals to bounce back from setbacks. This can be achieved through self-compassion, recognizing that everyone makes mistakes and experiences criticism. Embracing imperfection allows for a more balanced view of oneself and reduces the pressure to maintain a flawless self-image.

Furthermore, establishing a supportive network can enhance resilience. Engaging with friends, family, or support groups can provide a buffer against emotional upheavals, offering perspectives that encourage stability. Sharing experiences and challenges helps individuals feel less isolated and more understood, fostering a greater sense of belonging.

Continuous Growth

Finally, moving from reactivity to emotional stability is an ongoing process. Regular self-reflection, setting personal goals for emotional responses, and celebrating small victories along the way can reinforce positive changes. Establishing a routine that includes mindfulness, emotional regulation exercises, and supportive relationships will cultivate lasting emotional stability.

In summary, transitioning from reactivity to emotional stability is a transformative journey that requires self-awareness, emotional regulation, resilience, and continuous growth. With commitment and practice, individuals can develop a more balanced approach to their emotions, resulting in healthier relationships and a more fulfilling life.

Chapter 8

Self-Awareness: The Key to Transformation

The Role of Mindfulness in Self-Awareness

Mindfulness is the practice of being fully present and engaged in the moment, without judgment. This concept, deeply rooted in Buddhist traditions, has gained significant traction in modern psychology and self-help movements, particularly in the context of enhancing self-awareness. For individuals grappling with narcissistic traits, mindfulness can serve as a transformative tool, allowing for deeper introspection and a more accurate understanding of oneself.

Understanding Self-Awareness

Self-awareness involves recognizing one's thoughts, emotions, and behaviors and understanding how they influence oneself and others. It is the foundation of emotional intelligence and is crucial for personal growth and healthy relationships. For those who struggle with narcissism, self-awareness can be particularly challenging due to common traits such as defensiveness, a lack of empathy, and an overwhelming need for external validation. Mindfulness offers a pathway to break through these barriers.

Mindfulness Practices for Enhancing Self-Awareness

1. Mindful Breathing: This simple technique involves focusing on the breath as it enters and leaves the body. By anchoring attention to the breath, individuals can cultivate a sense of calm and clarity. This practice allows for the observation of thoughts without getting entangled in them, fostering an understanding of habitual thinking patterns that may be narcissistic in nature.

2. Body Scan Meditation: In this practice, individuals mentally scan their bodies from head to toe, paying attention to sensations, tension, and areas of discomfort. This creates a heightened awareness of physical manifestations of emotions, which can often be overlooked. By recognizing how feelings affect the body, individuals can develop a deeper connection between emotional experiences and narcissistic behaviors.

3. Journaling: Writing can be a powerful mindfulness tool. Keeping a daily journal allows individuals to reflect on their thoughts, feelings, and reactions in various situations. This reflective practice can help identify patterns of self-centered thinking and the triggers that lead to narcissistic responses, facilitating a deeper understanding of one's behaviors and their impact on relationships.

4. Mindful Observation: This technique encourages individuals to observe their surroundings and experiences without judgment. By practicing mindful observation, one can learn to appreciate the present moment and become more attuned to the feelings and needs of others, counteracting the self-absorption that often accompanies narcissism.

Developing Emotional Regulation through Mindfulness
Mindfulness also plays a critical role in emotional regulation. Narcissistic individuals often experience extreme reactions to perceived criticism or failure, leading to defensiveness or withdrawal. Mindfulness fosters emotional resilience by encouraging individuals to pause and reflect before reacting. This can help in recognizing the underlying fears or insecurities that drive narcissistic behaviors, allowing for more constructive responses to emotional challenges.

Cultivating Empathy through Mindfulness
An essential aspect of overcoming narcissism is developing empathy. Mindfulness enhances the ability to empathize by encouraging individuals to step outside their own experiences and consider others' perspectives. Mindfulness practices, such as loving-kindness meditation, specifically focus on promoting compassion towards oneself and others, thereby bridging the empathy gap often seen in narcissistic behavior.

Conclusion: A Path to Transformation
Incorporating mindfulness into daily life can significantly enhance self-awareness for those struggling with narcissistic traits. By fostering a non-judgmental attitude towards one's thoughts and feelings, mindfulness helps individuals understand their motivations and behaviors more clearly. This self-awareness is the first step towards personal growth, allowing for healthier relationships and a more fulfilling life. As individuals learn to navigate their inner worlds with greater clarity and compassion, they can begin to dismantle the patterns of narcissism that hinder both their well-being and their connections with others.

Practicing Self-Reflection: Journaling and Other Techniques
Self-reflection is an essential practice for anyone looking to understand themselves better and cultivate personal growth. In the context of narcissism, self-reflection serves as a powerful tool to break down self-centered behaviors and develop greater empathy and accountability. Engaging in self-reflection allows individuals to assess their thoughts, feelings, and actions, fostering deeper insights into their motivations and behaviors. Below, we explore various techniques for effective self-reflection, with a particular focus on journaling as a foundational

practice.

The Importance of Self-Reflection
Self-reflection is the process of examining one's own thoughts, feelings, and behaviors to gain insight into oneself. For individuals with narcissistic tendencies, self-reflection can be challenging but crucial for personal development. It enables individuals to recognize patterns in their behavior, including their responses to criticism, their need for validation, and their interactions with others. This awareness is the first step toward change, allowing individuals to move from a place of defensiveness to one of openness and growth.

Journaling as a Self-Reflection Tool
One of the most effective methods for engaging in self-reflection is journaling. This practice involves writing down thoughts, feelings, and experiences regularly, which can help clarify emotions and track personal growth. Here are several ways to incorporate journaling into self-reflection:

1. Daily Journaling: Set aside a few minutes each day to write about your thoughts and experiences. This can include reflections on your interactions with others, your emotional responses, and any insights you've gained throughout the day. By documenting your feelings and reactions, you can identify recurring themes and patterns that may indicate narcissistic tendencies.

2. Prompts for Reflection: Use specific prompts to guide your journaling sessions. Questions such as "What triggered my need for validation today?" or "How did I respond to criticism?" can encourage deeper exploration into your behaviors. This structured approach can help you focus your thoughts and make connections that might otherwise go unnoticed.

3. Gratitude Journaling: Practicing gratitude can shift the focus from self-centeredness to appreciation for others. Create a separate section in your journal dedicated to listing things you are grateful for each day. This can foster a sense of connectedness and humility, counteracting narcissistic tendencies by highlighting the positive aspects of your relationships with others.

4. Reflective Writing Exercises: Engage in longer writing exercises that explore significant experiences in your life. For instance, write about a conflict you had with someone and analyze your role in it. Consider how your actions may have impacted the other person and what you could have done differently. This kind of reflective writing promotes accountability and can lead to valuable insights.

Other Techniques for Self-Reflection

While journaling is a powerful tool, there are other techniques that can complement this practice:

- **Meditation and Mindfulness:** Practicing mindfulness can enhance self-awareness by encouraging you to observe your thoughts without judgment. Set aside time for meditation, focusing on your breath and allowing thoughts to come and go. This practice cultivates a sense of presence that can help you recognize and manage narcissistic impulses.

- **Feedback from Others:** Engaging in open conversations with trusted friends or family members can provide external perspectives on your behavior. Ask for constructive feedback about how you come across in social situations or how your actions affect others. This can be challenging but is invaluable for self-awareness.

- **Therapeutic Support:** Working with a therapist can offer guidance and support in your self-reflection journey. A professional can provide tools and frameworks to help you understand your behaviors and encourage accountability in a safe environment.

In conclusion, practicing self-reflection through journaling and other techniques is vital for personal growth, especially for those grappling with narcissistic tendencies. By committing to regular self-reflection, individuals can cultivate a deeper understanding of themselves, fostering healthier relationships and a more fulfilling life.

Developing Emotional Intelligence to Understand Your Feelings and Reactions

Emotional intelligence (EI) is the ability to recognize, understand, manage, and influence our own emotions and the emotions of others. It plays a critical role in personal development, particularly for those struggling with narcissistic tendencies, as it helps individuals navigate their own emotional landscape and cultivate healthier relationships. Developing emotional intelligence is not merely an academic exercise; it is a transformative process that enables individuals to better understand their feelings and reactions, fostering greater empathy and connection with others.

Understanding Emotions

At the heart of emotional intelligence is the ability to identify and understand emotions. This involves recognizing emotional triggers—situations or interactions that elicit specific feelings. For individuals with narcissistic traits, these triggers often stem from perceived threats to self-esteem or status, leading to defensive reactions. To develop emotional intelligence, one must engage in introspection to identify these triggers and their associated emotions, whether they be anger, shame, jealousy, or fear. Journaling can be a powerful tool in this process, allowing individuals to articulate their feelings and reflect on their emotional responses over time.

The Role of Self-Reflection

Self-reflection is essential for enhancing emotional intelligence. By regularly assessing one's emotional responses, individuals can begin to see patterns in their behavior and reactions. This practice encourages a deeper understanding of why certain situations evoke specific feelings, promoting self-awareness. For instance, if a person often feels rejected in social situations, reflecting on past experiences might reveal underlying fears of inadequacy or abandonment. By acknowledging these feelings and their origins, individuals can start to separate their self-worth from external validation and learn healthier coping mechanisms.

Emotional Regulation

Emotional intelligence also encompasses the ability to regulate one's emotions effectively. This means managing emotional responses in a way that is constructive rather than reactive. For those with narcissistic tendencies, learning to regulate emotions is crucial to avoid destructive behaviors such as lashing out or withdrawing when faced with criticism. Techniques such as mindfulness meditation can foster emotional regulation by teaching individuals to observe their thoughts and feelings without judgment. Through mindfulness, individuals can practice pausing before reacting, allowing them to respond thoughtfully rather than impulsively.

Empathy and Perspective-Taking

Another key component of emotional intelligence is empathy—the ability to understand and share the feelings of others. Developing empathy is particularly important for individuals struggling with narcissism, as it counters self-centered tendencies and promotes emotional connections. Engaging in perspective-taking exercises can help individuals step outside of their own experiences to appreciate others' feelings and viewpoints. For example, actively listening to a friend's concerns without immediately redirecting the conversation back to oneself fosters a sense of connection and understanding. Practicing empathy not only enhances relationships but also encourages a sense of community and belonging.

Seeking Feedback

Feedback from trusted friends, family, or therapists can also be instrumental in developing emotional intelligence. Constructive feedback provides outside perspectives on one's emotional responses and behaviors, illuminating areas for growth. When receiving feedback, it is essential to approach it with an open mind—viewing it as an opportunity for improvement rather than a personal attack. This openness to feedback cultivates a growth mindset, reinforcing the understanding that emotional intelligence is not a fixed trait but a skill that can be developed over time.

Conclusion

In conclusion, developing emotional intelligence is a vital journey for anyone looking to understand their feelings and reactions better, especially those grappling with narcissistic traits. By focusing on self-reflection, emotional regulation, empathy, and seeking feedback, individuals can foster a deeper connection with themselves and others. This process not only aids in personal growth but also paves the way for healthier, more fulfilling relationships, ultimately leading to a more balanced and empathetic life.

Embracing Feedback and Constructive Criticism

Embracing feedback and constructive criticism is a vital step in overcoming narcissistic tendencies and fostering personal growth. Individuals with narcissistic traits often struggle to accept feedback due to their heightened sensitivity to perceived criticism, which can trigger defensive mechanisms and emotional reactivity. This defensiveness can manifest as anger, denial, or even withdrawal, impeding the opportunity for meaningful self-reflection and development. To transition toward a healthier mindset, it is essential to cultivate an openness to feedback that can serve as a catalyst for transformation.

Understanding the Value of Feedback

Feedback is an invaluable tool for growth, providing insights into how our actions and behaviors are perceived by others. Constructive criticism is not an attack on our character but rather a means of highlighting areas for improvement. It can illuminate blind spots, revealing patterns that we may be unaware of and offering perspectives that can enhance our interpersonal relationships. By embracing feedback, we open ourselves to learning opportunities that can ultimately lead to greater self-awareness and emotional intelligence.

Reframing the Narrative Around Criticism

One of the first steps in embracing feedback is to reframe the narrative surrounding criticism. Instead of viewing feedback as a personal affront, it can be helpful to see it as an essential part of the learning process. This mindset shift allows individuals to approach criticism with curiosity rather than defensiveness. When feedback is perceived as a gift aimed at fostering growth, it becomes easier to accept and integrate into our personal development journey.

Practicing Active Listening

Active listening is a crucial skill in the process of embracing feedback. This involves being fully present during conversations, focusing on the speaker's words without formulating a response while they are talking. By practicing active listening, individuals can better understand the feedback being offered and demonstrate respect for the perspectives of others. This practice not only enhances comprehension but also fosters a sense of connection and empathy, vital components in building lasting relationships.

Accepting Feedback Without Immediate Reaction

When receiving feedback, it's natural to feel an emotional response. However, it is important to practice restraint and avoid reacting impulsively. Taking a moment to breathe and process the information allows individuals to respond thoughtfully rather than defensively. Journaling about the feedback received can also help in processing emotions and reflecting on the validity of the critique without the pressure of an immediate response.

Seeking Clarification and Asking Questions

If feedback is vague or unclear, seeking clarification is a constructive step. Asking open-ended questions can provide deeper insights into the feedback and demonstrate a genuine interest in understanding the other person's perspective. This approach not only helps in grasping the intent behind the criticism but also reinforces a commitment to personal growth.

Developing a Growth Mindset

Adopting a growth mindset is integral to embracing feedback. This perspective emphasizes that abilities and intelligence can be developed through dedication and hard work. Individuals with a growth mindset view challenges, including criticism, as opportunities to learn and grow. By fostering this mindset, individuals can more readily accept feedback and use it to propel their personal development.

Reflecting on Feedback and Setting Intentions

After receiving feedback, it's essential to reflect on it thoughtfully. Consider how the feedback aligns with personal goals and values. Setting specific intentions based on the feedback can create a roadmap for growth, making it easier to track progress and stay committed to change. This process not only reinforces accountability but also allows for a proactive approach to personal development.

Conclusion

Embracing feedback and constructive criticism is a challenging yet crucial aspect of personal growth for those grappling with narcissistic tendencies. By reframing our relationship with feedback, practicing active listening, and cultivating a growth mindset, we can transform criticism into a powerful tool for self-improvement. Ultimately, this practice fosters healthier relationships, deeper connections, and a more fulfilling, empathetic life.

Tracking Personal Growth: Measuring Progress Over Time

Personal growth is a continuous journey characterized by self-discovery, learning, and transformation. For individuals seeking to address narcissistic traits, measuring progress is an essential component of the healing process. By tracking personal growth, individuals can gain insights into their behaviors, thoughts, and feelings, helping to establish a clear understanding of their evolution over time. This section outlines effective strategies for monitoring personal development, setting meaningful goals, and celebrating achievements in the quest for a healthier, more balanced life.

The Importance of Self-Reflection

Self-reflection is a foundational practice for tracking personal growth. It involves taking time to contemplate one's actions, thoughts, and emotional responses. Regular self-reflection can be facilitated through journaling, meditation, or structured self-assessment exercises. Journaling, in particular, serves as a powerful tool for documenting experiences, emotions, and insights. By reviewing past entries, individuals can identify patterns, recognize shifts in perspective, and celebrate milestones in their journey toward healing.

Setting Measurable Goals

To effectively measure progress, it is vital to establish clear, achievable goals. SMART goals—Specific, Measurable, Achievable, Relevant, and Time-bound—provide a framework for defining objectives related to personal growth. For instance, if an individual seeks to cultivate empathy, they might set a goal to engage in three acts of kindness each week or practice active listening in conversations. By breaking down larger aspirations into smaller, manageable goals, individuals can create a roadmap for success and easily assess their advancement over time.

Utilizing Feedback

Feedback from trusted friends, family members, or mental health professionals can offer valuable insights into personal growth. Individuals should seek constructive feedback regarding their behaviors and interactions, especially in relation to narcissistic tendencies. Engaging in open conversations about personal growth can help identify blind spots and highlight areas for further improvement. Furthermore, embracing feedback can foster a growth mindset, reinforcing the understanding that personal development is an ongoing process rather than a destination.

Tracking Emotional Responses
Emotional awareness plays a significant role in personal growth. By tracking emotional responses to various situations, individuals can gain a deeper understanding of their triggers and patterns of behavior. Maintaining an emotional log—documenting feelings, reactions, and the context of emotional experiences—can help individuals identify recurring themes and measure their progress over time. For example, if someone previously reacted defensively to criticism but gradually learns to respond with understanding, this shift can be documented and celebrated as a significant step forward.

Celebrating Milestones
Recognizing and celebrating milestones is crucial for maintaining motivation and reinforcing positive changes. Personal growth often occurs in small increments, and acknowledging these achievements—no matter how minor—can boost self-esteem and encourage continued progress. Milestones can include successfully navigating a challenging conversation, practicing vulnerability, or demonstrating increased empathy in interactions. Creating a visual representation of progress, such as a growth chart or a gratitude jar, can serve as a tangible reminder of achievements.

Reflection and Adjustment
Tracking personal growth is not a static process; it requires ongoing reflection and adjustment. As individuals evolve, their goals and strategies may need to be recalibrated to align with their current state of being. Regularly revisiting and revising goals ensures that they remain relevant and challenging. This adaptability is essential to sustaining momentum in the journey toward overcoming narcissistic traits and fostering healthier relationships.

In conclusion, tracking personal growth is an integral aspect of healing from narcissistic behaviors. Through self-reflection, goal-setting, feedback, emotional tracking, and celebration of milestones, individuals can measure their progress meaningfully and cultivate a more empathetic and fulfilling life. This iterative process not only enhances self-awareness but also promotes resilience and a deeper connection with oneself and others.

Chapter 9

Transforming Narcissistic Habits

Shifting from Self-Centeredness to Serving Others

The transition from a self-centered perspective to one that emphasizes serving others is a profound journey that can have a transformative impact on personal growth and relationships. At the core of this shift lies the recognition that true fulfillment and joy often stem from our connections with others, rather than from the pursuit of self-aggrandizement or external validation.

Understanding Self-Centeredness

Self-centeredness is often rooted in a narcissistic mindset that prioritizes personal desires, achievements, and recognition. Individuals exhibiting self-centered behaviors may find themselves constantly seeking admiration and validation, often at the expense of others. This fixation can lead to feelings of isolation and dissatisfaction, as relationships become transactional rather than meaningful. Recognizing these patterns is the first step toward change.

The Benefits of Serving Others

Shifting focus from oneself to serving others can lead to numerous emotional and psychological benefits. When we engage in acts of kindness and service, we experience a sense of purpose and fulfillment. Research has shown that helping others can enhance our own well-being, reduce stress, and even improve our physical health. Serving others fosters empathy, deepens connections, and cultivates a sense of community, all of which contribute to a more balanced and happy life.

Practical Steps to Shift Focus

1. Cultivating Empathy: One of the fundamental aspects of serving others is developing empathy. Empathy involves understanding and sharing the feelings of others, which can be cultivated through active listening and perspective-taking. By putting ourselves in someone else's shoes, we begin to appreciate their struggles and joys, which naturally shifts our focus away from our own needs.

2. Engaging in Volunteer Work: Participating in community service or volunteer opportunities provides practical avenues to serve others. Whether it's assisting at a local food bank, mentoring youth, or engaging in environmental clean-up efforts, these activities not only help those in need but also create a sense of belonging and purpose for the volunteer.

3. Practicing Gratitude: Gratitude shifts the focus from what we lack to what we have. By regularly reflecting on the positive aspects of our lives and expressing appreciation for them, we cultivate a mindset that recognizes the contributions of others. Keeping a gratitude journal can help reinforce this practice, encouraging us to acknowledge those who positively impact our lives.

4. Building Genuine Relationships: Serving others often begins with fostering genuine relationships. Invest time in getting to know friends, family, and colleagues on a deeper level. Show genuine interest in their lives, listen actively, and offer support when needed. As these relationships strengthen, the desire to serve and support each other naturally grows.

5. Setting Intentional Goals: Shift your personal goals to include service-oriented objectives. This could be committing to a certain number of volunteer hours per month or finding ways to support colleagues at work. Intentionality in setting these goals can help reinforce the habit of serving others.

6. Mindfulness and Reflection: Regular mindfulness practices can enhance self-awareness, allowing individuals to identify moments of self-centered thinking. Engaging in reflective practices, such as journaling about one's thoughts and behaviors, can help track progress and reinforce the commitment to serving others.

7. Creating a Culture of Service: Encourage a culture of service in personal and professional environments by promoting teamwork and collaboration. Recognize and celebrate acts of kindness and service among peers, reinforcing the idea that serving others is a shared value.

In conclusion, shifting from self-centeredness to serving others is not merely a change in behavior but a transformation of mindset. As individuals embrace service, they not only enhance their own lives but also contribute positively to their communities and relationships. This shift not only enriches one's sense of purpose but also fosters a more compassionate and interconnected world.

Creating a Daily Practice of Gratitude and Generosity

In the journey to understand and mitigate narcissistic tendencies, fostering a daily practice of gratitude and generosity can serve as a powerful antidote. These practices not only cultivate a sense of fulfillment and connection but also shift the focus away from self-centeredness, encouraging a more expansive view of one's experiences and relationships.

The Importance of Gratitude

Gratitude is more than just a fleeting feeling; it's a profound practice that can reshape the way individuals perceive their lives. Numerous studies have demonstrated the psychological benefits of gratitude, including improved mood, increased resilience, and enhanced overall well-being. When individuals consciously acknowledge and appreciate the positive aspects of their lives, they cultivate an attitude of abundance rather than scarcity.

To cultivate gratitude, consider implementing the following strategies:

1. Gratitude Journaling: Dedicate a few minutes each day to write down three to five things you are grateful for. These can be as simple as a warm cup of coffee or as significant as a supportive friend. Over time, this practice helps rewire the brain to focus on positive experiences.

2. Daily Affirmations: Incorporate affirmations that center around gratitude. For instance, phrases like "I am thankful for the love in my life" or "I appreciate the beauty around me" can shift your mindset throughout the day.

3. Mindful Moments: Set aside time for mindfulness, where you consciously reflect on what you appreciate in your life. This could be done during meditation, while taking a walk, or even during mundane tasks.

The Role of Generosity

Generosity is another critical aspect of this practice. Engaging in acts of kindness not only benefits others but also reinforces the giver's sense of purpose and connection. Generosity can take many forms, from small gestures to larger commitments, and each act contributes to a culture of empathy and community.

Consider these approaches to incorporate generosity into your daily life:

1. Random Acts of Kindness: Challenge yourself to perform at least one act of kindness each day. This could be as simple as holding the door for someone, complimenting a coworker, or leaving a positive note for a friend.

2. Volunteering: Identify causes that resonate with you and dedicate time to volunteer. Whether it's at a local food bank, an animal shelter, or a community center, giving your time can create meaningful connections and foster a sense of belonging.

3. Sharing Resources: Consider sharing your skills or knowledge with others. This could involve tutoring someone in a subject you excel in, providing mentorship, or even sharing tools and resources you have with neighbors or friends.

The Interconnection of Gratitude and Generosity

Embracing gratitude and generosity creates a virtuous cycle. When you express gratitude, you become more aware of the positive influences in your life, which can inspire you to give back. Conversely, acts of generosity often lead to feelings of satisfaction and joy, enhancing your overall sense of gratitude.

To ensure these practices become an integral part of your daily routine, consider setting reminders on your phone or incorporating them into existing habits, such as during your morning coffee or before bedtime. The goal is to create a mindset where gratitude and generosity become second nature—an automatic response to life's challenges and opportunities.

By establishing a daily practice of gratitude and generosity, you not only enrich your own life but also contribute positively to the lives of those around you. This shift toward an outward focus diminishes narcissistic tendencies, paving the way for a more empathetic, connected, and fulfilling existence. In essence, creating this practice is a transformative step towards healing and personal growth, fostering a life that values connection over isolation.

Learning to Accept Criticism and Grow from It

Accepting criticism can be one of the most challenging aspects of personal growth, particularly for individuals with narcissistic tendencies. Narcissism often manifests as a need for validation and a fear of inadequacy, making it difficult to receive feedback without feeling attacked. However, learning to accept criticism constructively is essential for emotional maturity, relationship health, and personal development. This section explores the importance of accepting criticism, strategies to do so effectively, and the potential for growth that comes from embracing this often-uncomfortable process.

Understanding the Nature of Criticism

Criticism can be broadly categorized into constructive and destructive forms. Constructive criticism is intended to provide helpful feedback aimed at fostering improvement, while destructive criticism is often meant to belittle or demean. Understanding this distinction is crucial for developing a healthy perspective on feedback. Constructive criticism, when delivered appropriately, serves as a tool for self-improvement.

Individuals with narcissistic traits may react defensively when faced with criticism, interpreting it as a personal attack rather than an opportunity for growth. This reaction is rooted in the fear of exposure and vulnerability, which narcissistic individuals typically avoid. Recognizing that criticism is a normal part of life and does not diminish one's self-worth is the first step toward accepting it.

Strategies for Accepting Criticism

1. Mindfulness and Emotional Awareness: Practicing mindfulness can help individuals become more aware of their emotional responses to criticism. By observing feelings of defensiveness or anger without judgment, one can begin to create a space for reflection rather than reaction. Over time, this practice can lead to a more measured response to feedback.

2. Reframing the Message: Instead of viewing criticism as a negative reflection of personal worth, it can be helpful to reframe it as an opportunity for growth. Ask yourself, "What can I learn from this feedback?" This shift in perspective can make criticism feel less threatening and more like an invitation to improve.

3. Seek Specific Feedback: When receiving criticism, especially in professional or personal relationships, it can be beneficial to ask for specific examples. This approach clarifies the feedback and allows for targeted action rather than vague feelings of inadequacy. For instance, instead of simply hearing "You did a poor job," one might ask, "Can you explain which areas I could improve upon?"

4. Practice Gratitude for Feedback: Developing a sense of gratitude for those who offer constructive criticism can shift the emotional landscape around feedback. Recognize that those providing feedback often have your best interests at heart. Expressing gratitude, even internally, can help mitigate feelings of defensiveness.

5. Cultivating a Growth Mindset: Embracing a growth mindset involves the belief that abilities and intelligence can be developed with effort over time. This perspective allows individuals to view criticism as a pathway for growth rather than a fixed judgment of their capabilities.

The Growth That Follows
Accepting criticism is not merely about tolerating it but actively engaging with it to foster personal development. Each piece of constructive feedback provides an opportunity to reflect, learn, and adjust behaviors or perspectives. Over time, this practice can lead to enhanced self-awareness, improved relationships, and greater overall emotional resilience.

Moreover, learning to accept criticism can significantly improve interpersonal dynamics. When individuals respond to feedback with openness rather than defensiveness, they create a culture of trust and vulnerability in their relationships, allowing for deeper connections and more meaningful interactions.

In conclusion, while accepting criticism can be challenging, it is a vital skill that contributes to personal growth and relational health. By employing mindfulness techniques, reframing feedback, seeking specificity, practicing gratitude, and cultivating a growth mindset, individuals can learn to not only accept criticism but also thrive because of it. Embracing feedback as a tool for development opens the door to a more fulfilling, emotionally intelligent life.

Moving from Self-Promotion to Humility
In a culture that often equates success with visibility and recognition, the impulse to self-promote can be overwhelming. Narcissistic tendencies thrive in environments that reward self-aggrandizement, leading individuals to prioritize personal achievements over genuine connections with others. However, transitioning from self-promotion to humility is essential for personal growth, emotional well-being, and building meaningful relationships. This section explores the importance of humility, the pitfalls of self-promotion, and actionable strategies for cultivating a humble mindset.

Understanding Humility
Humility is often misconstrued as a lack of self-worth or an inability to recognize one's strengths. In truth, humility is an understanding of one's place in the broader context of life. It involves acknowledging one's abilities and achievements while also recognizing the contributions of others and the interdependence that exists in human relationships. Humility allows for an authentic sense of self that is not contingent upon external validation, fostering genuine interactions and deeper connections.

The Pitfalls of Self-Promotion
Self-promotion can lead to a range of issues, both internally and externally. Internally, the persistent need for validation can create a fragile self-esteem that relies on external approval. This dependence makes individuals vulnerable to criticism and rejection, often resulting in a cycle of anxiety and defensive behavior. Externally, constant self-promotion can alienate others,

leading to superficial relationships where genuine connection is sacrificed for the sake of image.

Moreover, self-promotion often breeds a competitive mindset that views others not as collaborators but as rivals. This perspective can stifle teamwork and collaboration, undermining the collective efforts necessary for personal and professional success.

Strategies for Cultivating Humility

1. Practice Gratitude: One of the most effective ways to foster humility is by regularly engaging in gratitude practices. Taking the time to reflect on the contributions of others in your life can shift your focus from self to community. Keeping a gratitude journal, where you note the people and experiences for which you are thankful, can help reinforce this mindset.

2. Embrace Vulnerability: Vulnerability is a cornerstone of humility. Sharing your struggles and acknowledging your imperfections invites authenticity into your relationships. It allows others to see you as a whole person, fostering deeper connections. Engage in conversations where you can express your challenges and learn from others' experiences.

3. Seek Feedback: Embracing feedback is crucial for moving away from self-promotion. Actively seek constructive criticism from trusted individuals in your life. Approach these conversations with an open mind, viewing feedback as an opportunity for growth rather than a personal attack. This practice cultivates a mindset that values learning over validation.

4. Shift the Focus: Make a conscious effort to shift the focus of conversations away from yourself. Ask open-ended questions that invite others to share their experiences and perspectives. This not only allows you to learn from others but also reinforces the value of their contributions, fostering a more collaborative environment.

5. Celebrate Others: Make it a habit to celebrate the achievements and strengths of others. Whether it's a colleague's success at work or a friend's accomplishment in their personal life, publicly acknowledging their successes promotes an atmosphere of support and appreciation. This practice diminishes the need for self-promotion by creating a culture of mutual respect.

6. Reflect Regularly: Set aside time for self-reflection, examining your motivations and behaviors. Journaling can be a powerful tool in this process. Ask yourself questions like, "What drives my need to share my achievements?" or "How can I contribute to the success of others?" This practice fosters self-awareness, allowing you to recognize and adjust self-promotional tendencies.

Conclusion
Transitioning from self-promotion to humility is a journey that involves intentional effort and self-reflection. By embracing gratitude, vulnerability, and collaboration, individuals can cultivate genuine relationships and foster a deeper sense of self-worth that is not reliant on external validation. Ultimately, humility not only enriches personal lives but also contributes to a more compassionate and interconnected society.

Sustaining Long-Term Change
Sustaining long-term change, particularly in the context of overcoming narcissistic tendencies, is a multifaceted process that requires commitment, self-awareness, and the establishment of healthy habits. While the journey toward personal growth and emotional health may begin with a series of insights and revelations, the real challenge lies in maintaining these changes over time. Here are several key strategies to ensure that the positive transformations you initiate become enduring aspects of your life.

1. Establishing Consistent Practices
One of the most effective ways to sustain change is to create consistent daily practices that reinforce your new behaviors and thought patterns. **This could include:**

- **Mindfulness Meditation:** Engaging in mindfulness practice can help you remain present and aware of your thoughts and feelings, allowing you to recognize narcissistic patterns as they arise. Regular meditation fosters emotional regulation and self-reflection, which are essential for long-term change.

- **Gratitude Journaling:** Keeping a gratitude journal helps shift your focus from self-centeredness to appreciation for others and the world around you. By regularly noting things you are thankful for, you cultivate a sense of humility and interconnectedness.

- **Daily Self-Reflection:** Set aside time each day for self-reflection, where you can assess your thoughts and behaviors. Journaling or using prompts can guide you in evaluating how your actions align with your goals for personal growth.

2. Building a Supportive Community
Surrounding yourself with a supportive community is vital for sustaining change. Engaging with others who understand your journey fosters accountability and encouragement. Consider:

- **Therapy or Support Groups:** Participating in therapy, especially group therapy, can provide you with a safe space to share experiences and learn from others who are on similar paths. A therapist can guide you in navigating challenges and celebrating milestones.

- **Accountability Partners:** Identify friends or family members who can act as accountability partners. Regular check-ins can help you stay committed to your goals and provide motivation when you feel discouraged.

3. Setting Realistic Goals

Sustained change is often more achievable when you set realistic and measurable goals. Break larger goals into smaller, manageable steps. This approach not only makes the process less overwhelming but also allows you to celebrate small victories along the way. For example:

- **Short-Term Goals:** Focus on daily or weekly objectives that align with your overarching goals for personal growth, such as practicing empathy or managing your reactions in challenging situations.

- **Long-Term Goals:** Establish broader, long-term goals that you can work toward over months or years, like improving your relationships or enhancing your emotional intelligence.

4. Embracing Flexibility

Change is not a linear process, and setbacks are a natural part of growth. Embrace flexibility and be open to adjusting your strategies as needed. When faced with challenges, practice self-compassion rather than self-criticism. Recognize that growth often involves ups and downs, and it's okay to seek help or reassess your approach when necessary.

5. Celebrating Progress

Regularly take time to celebrate your progress, no matter how small. Acknowledging your achievements reinforces positive behaviors and motivates you to continue on your path. Consider creating a visual representation of your growth, such as a progress chart or a list of successes, to remind yourself of how far you've come.

6. Continuously Learning

Finally, commit to lifelong learning. Read self-help books, attend workshops, and engage in activities that promote personal growth and emotional intelligence. Staying informed about narcissism and its impacts can help you maintain awareness of your own behaviors and the importance of empathy and connection.

By integrating these strategies into your life, you can create a sustainable framework for personal transformation that not only diminishes narcissistic tendencies but also fosters a fulfilling and authentic existence. The journey toward sustained change is ongoing, and with dedication and support, it is entirely achievable.

Chapter 10

Healthy Boundaries: Learning to Respect Others

Understanding the Importance of Boundaries in Relationships

Boundaries are essential components of healthy relationships, acting as invisible lines that define personal limits, protect individual rights, and foster mutual respect. In the context of narcissism—where self-centeredness often overshadows empathy—understanding and establishing boundaries becomes even more crucial. This section delves into why boundaries matter and how they can transform interactions within relationships, particularly those affected by narcissistic traits.

Defining Boundaries

Boundaries can be understood as guidelines that dictate how we allow others to treat us and how we engage with them. They encompass emotional, physical, and psychological dimensions. Emotional boundaries involve understanding and respecting feelings, while physical boundaries define personal space and physical touch. Psychological boundaries protect one's thoughts, beliefs, and self-esteem, ensuring that one's identity remains intact amidst external pressures.

The Role of Boundaries in Relationships

1. Protection: Boundaries act as a protective barrier against emotional harm and manipulation. In relationships with narcissistic individuals, where gaslighting or emotional abuse may occur, establishing clear boundaries can help safeguard personal integrity and mental health. Without boundaries, individuals may find themselves trapped in cycles of blame, guilt, and self-doubt.

2. Clarity: Setting boundaries provides clarity in relationships. They communicate expectations and limit behaviors that are unacceptable. For instance, if a partner continually belittles or criticizes, clearly stating that such behavior is not tolerable helps define the parameters of respect and kindness. This clarity can prompt narcissistic individuals to reflect on their actions and potentially alter their behavior, fostering healthier interactions.

3. Self-Respect: Establishing boundaries is an act of self-respect. It signals to both oneself and others that one values their own needs and feelings. In relationships where narcissism is present, individuals often sacrifice their own well-being to accommodate the narcissistic partner. By asserting boundaries, a person reclaims their sense of self-worth and reinforces the idea that their feelings are valid and significant.

4. Encouraging Mutual Respect: Healthy boundaries promote mutual respect in relationships. They encourage open communication and enable both parties to express their needs without fear of aggression or manipulation. When both partners understand and respect each other's limits, the relationship can thrive on a foundation of trust and empathy.

5. Facilitating Personal Growth: Boundaries are essential for personal growth and emotional well-being. They create a space for individuals to explore their thoughts and feelings independently of external influence. For those dealing with narcissistic traits, boundaries can help in recognizing the difference between healthy self-assertion and unhealthy self-centeredness. Individuals can learn to prioritize their own needs while still being considerate of others, fostering a balanced approach to relationships.

Setting Personal Boundaries Without Guilt

Establishing boundaries often comes with feelings of guilt or fear of conflict, especially in relationships where narcissism is prevalent. However, it is vital to understand that setting boundaries is not a selfish act; rather, it is a necessary step to ensure a healthy relational dynamic. Here are some strategies for setting boundaries effectively:

- **Communicate Clearly:** Be direct and specific about your boundaries. Use "I" statements to express how certain behaviors affect you. For example, "I feel overwhelmed when you interrupt me during conversations" conveys a personal experience without accusatory language.

- **Stay Consistent:** Consistency reinforces boundaries. If a boundary is crossed, calmly remind the individual of the established limit. Consistent enforcement is key to ensuring that boundaries are respected over time.

- **Practice Self-Care:** Prioritize self-care to maintain emotional balance. Engage in activities that rejuvenate you and build resilience against potential boundary violations.

- **Seek Support:** In challenging relationships, seeking support from friends, family, or a therapist can provide validation and guidance in maintaining boundaries.

In summary, boundaries are not merely restrictions; they are essential frameworks that nurture respect, clarity, and personal growth in relationships. For individuals grappling with narcissism—whether in themselves or in others—understanding and implementing boundaries can be transformative, leading to healthier, more fulfilling connections.

Setting Personal Boundaries Without Guilt

Setting personal boundaries is a crucial component of maintaining healthy relationships and fostering personal well-being. Yet, many individuals, especially those grappling with narcissistic tendencies or traits, often struggle with this essential skill due to feelings of guilt. The process of establishing boundaries can feel uncomfortable, leading to internal conflicts that make individuals question their right to assert their needs. However, it is important to understand that setting boundaries is not only an act of self-care but also a vital step in cultivating respectful interactions with others.

Understanding Boundaries

Boundaries define where one person ends and another begins. They help establish a clear line regarding what is acceptable and what is not, both in terms of behavior and emotional space. Healthy boundaries can encompass physical, emotional, and psychological aspects. Recognizing the importance of boundaries is the first step toward understanding how they can enhance the quality of your relationships.

The Guilt Factor

Feelings of guilt often arise when we consider asserting our boundaries, leading to a cycle of self-doubt and fear of confrontation. This guilt can stem from various sources, including cultural conditioning, childhood experiences, or a deep-seated belief that prioritizing one's needs is selfish. It's vital to challenge these beliefs and acknowledge that establishing boundaries is an act of self-respect and not an affront to others.

Reframing Your Mindset

To set boundaries without guilt, start by reframing your mindset. Recognize that your needs and feelings are valid. It can be helpful to adopt the perspective that healthy relationships are built on mutual respect, and that includes respecting your own needs. Remind yourself that boundaries are not walls but rather guidelines that enable more authentic interactions. When you establish boundaries, you create space for honesty, trust, and deeper connections.

Practical Steps to Set Boundaries

1. Identify Your Limits: Take time to reflect on your personal limits. What behaviors from others make you feel uncomfortable or drained? Understanding your emotional responses will help you articulate your needs.

2. Communicate Clearly: Once you've identified your boundaries, communicate them clearly and assertively to others. Use "I" statements to express your feelings without placing blame. For example, "I feel overwhelmed when…" rather than "You always…"

3. Practice Assertiveness: Being assertive is crucial when setting boundaries. It means expressing your needs confidently while respecting the needs of others. Practice saying no without over-explaining or justifying your decision.

4. Be Consistent: Once you've set your boundaries, be consistent in enforcing them. Inconsistency can lead others to question your limits and may undermine your efforts. If someone crosses a boundary, address it promptly and reaffirm your limits.

5. Prepare for Reactions: Understand that not everyone will respond positively to your boundaries. Some may feel surprised, upset, or even angry. Remind yourself that their reaction is not your responsibility, and it's a natural part of the process.

6. Self-Compassion: It's essential to practice self-compassion as you navigate boundary-setting. Acknowledge that it's okay to prioritize your needs and that doing so fosters healthier relationships. Treat yourself with the same kindness you would offer a friend in a similar situation.

Moving Forward

Setting personal boundaries is an ongoing practice. As you become more comfortable with asserting your needs, the guilt associated with boundary-setting will diminish. Remember that boundaries are not about shutting others out but about creating a safe space for both yourself and others. By prioritizing your emotional well-being, you pave the way for more authentic, fulfilling connections, ultimately leading to healthier relationships and a more balanced life. Embrace the journey of boundary-setting as a vital step toward personal growth and emotional health.

Recognizing and Respecting the Boundaries of Others

Boundaries are essential to maintaining healthy relationships, as they define where one person ends and another begins. Recognizing and respecting the boundaries of others is particularly vital in relationships involving individuals with narcissistic traits, as these individuals often struggle with understanding the personal limits of others. This section delves into the significance of boundaries, the challenges narcissistic individuals face in recognizing them, and practical strategies for fostering mutual respect in relationships.

Understanding Boundaries

Boundaries come in various forms: physical, emotional, and social. Physical boundaries relate to personal space and physical touch; emotional boundaries involve the feelings and thoughts we share with others; social boundaries pertain to our interactions with others, including how we choose to spend our time and energy. Recognizing these boundaries is key to fostering respect and empathy in all types of relationships—romantic, familial, and friendships.

When boundaries are respected, relationships thrive. Individuals feel safe and valued, leading to healthier communication and emotional connection. Conversely, when boundaries are violated, feelings of resentment, discomfort, and mistrust can arise, potentially leading to toxic dynamics.

Challenges for Narcissistic Individuals

Individuals exhibiting narcissistic traits may struggle significantly with recognizing and respecting the boundaries of others. This difficulty often stems from a combination of self-centeredness and a lack of empathy. Narcissists may prioritize their own needs and desires above those of others, leading to boundary violations that can manifest in various ways, such as:

1. Disregarding Personal Space: Narcissists might invade personal space without regard for others' comfort, often viewing such behavior as a means to assert dominance or control.

2. Overstepping Emotional Boundaries: They may fail to consider the emotional impact of their words and actions, leading to manipulative behaviors or emotional exploitation.

3. Neglecting Social Boundaries: Narcissists may demand excessive time and attention from others, disregarding their partners' or friends' need for personal time, independence, or social engagements outside the relationship.

Strategies for Recognizing and Respecting Boundaries

1. Self-Reflection and Awareness: Narcissistic individuals must engage in self-reflection to understand their own tendencies to overstep boundaries. Acknowledging these patterns is the first step toward change.

2. Active Listening: Practice active listening to understand the needs and limits of others. This involves not only hearing their words but also paying attention to their body language and emotional cues.

3. Clear Communication: Encourage open dialogue about boundaries. Express your own needs and limitations clearly and invite others to share theirs. This fosters an environment of respect and understanding.

4. Learning to Say No: Understand that it's acceptable to say no to requests that infringe on your boundaries. For narcissistic individuals, this may involve learning to tolerate discomfort when their demands are not met.

5. Empathy Building: Cultivating empathy is crucial for recognizing the boundaries of others. Techniques such as perspective-taking—considering how someone else may feel in a given situation—can enhance empathetic understanding.

6. Practicing Patience: Recognizing and respecting boundaries is not an overnight process. It requires patience, practice, and a commitment to personal growth.

7. Seeking Feedback: Actively seek feedback from trusted friends or family members about boundary interactions. This can provide valuable insights into how your behaviors affect others.

Conclusion
Recognizing and respecting the boundaries of others is integral to building and maintaining healthy relationships. For individuals with narcissistic traits, developing this awareness involves a commitment to personal growth, empathy, and self-reflection. By taking proactive steps to understand and honor the limits of others, individuals can foster deeper connections and cultivate a more respectful and supportive interpersonal environment. This journey not only enhances relationships but also contributes to the individual's overall emotional health and well-being.

Dealing with Boundary Violations in a Healthy Way
Navigating relationships, whether personal or professional, involves establishing and maintaining boundaries. Boundaries are essential for healthy interactions, as they delineate where one person ends and another begins. When boundaries are crossed, it can lead to feelings of discomfort, resentment, and even emotional turmoil. Learning how to deal with boundary violations in a healthy way is crucial for fostering self-respect and improving interpersonal relationships.

Understanding Boundary Violations
A boundary violation occurs when someone disregards the limits you've set regarding your personal space, emotions, time, or resources. These violations can be physical, emotional, or even psychological. For instance, a friend who constantly interrupts your personal time or a colleague who tries to undermine your authority can create an unhealthy environment that fosters resentment and insecurity.

Recognizing boundary violations is the first step towards addressing them effectively. It's important to be aware of your own boundaries and to understand when they have been crossed. This self-awareness allows you to respond rather than react impulsively, which can often exacerbate the situation.

Assessing the Situation

When a boundary violation occurs, take a moment to assess the situation. Ask yourself the following questions:

1. What boundary was violated? Identify the specific limit that was disregarded. Is it related to your time, emotional space, or physical presence?

2. How did it make you feel? Acknowledge your emotions—whether it's anger, sadness, or frustration—recognizing these feelings is vital for understanding the impact of the violation.

3. Was it intentional or unintentional? Consider the other person's intent. Sometimes, people may not be aware that they are crossing a boundary. Understanding their perspective can inform how you choose to address the issue.

Communicating Your Boundaries

Once you've assessed the situation, it's essential to communicate your boundaries clearly and assertively. This is where many people struggle; however, effective communication is key to maintaining healthy relationships. Here are some strategies:

- **Be Direct:** Use clear and concise language to express your feelings. For example, instead of saying, "I don't like when you do that," you might say, "I feel uncomfortable when you interrupt me during discussions."
- **Use "I" Statements:** Frame your feelings around your experiences. This reduces defensiveness in the other person. For instance, "I feel overwhelmed when plans change at the last minute" is more effective than "You always change plans without notice."
- **Stay Calm and Composed:** Emotions can run high during these conversations. Practice staying calm and composed, which will help you communicate more effectively.

Setting Consequences

If boundary violations persist despite your efforts to communicate, it may be necessary to establish consequences. Boundaries are not merely suggestions; they require respect and compliance. You might say, "If this continues, I will need to take a step back from our relationship." Setting consequences not only protects you but also communicates the seriousness of your boundaries.

Seeking Support
Sometimes, it can be beneficial to seek support from friends, family, or a therapist. They can provide you with perspective and strategies for handling boundary violations. Additionally, if the violations continue, professional help can assist in navigating the complexities of relationships with individuals who may struggle with understanding boundaries.

Practicing Self-Care
Finally, dealing with boundary violations can be emotionally taxing. Engage in self-care practices that restore your emotional well-being. This could include mindfulness exercises, journaling, or spending time in nature. Practicing self-care helps reinforce your self-worth and empowers you to maintain your boundaries effectively.

In conclusion, dealing with boundary violations in a healthy way involves recognizing the violation, assessing the situation, communicating your needs clearly, and, if necessary, establishing consequences. By prioritizing your boundaries, you foster respect in your relationships, paving the way for healthier interactions and a more balanced life.

Balancing Self-Care and Responsibility in Relationships
In the realm of personal development, especially for individuals grappling with narcissistic tendencies, the balance between self-care and responsibility in relationships can be particularly challenging. This balance is essential not only for the health of the individual but also for the well-being of their relationships. Recognizing the importance of self-care while also acknowledging the responsibilities we have toward others can foster healthier interactions and promote emotional growth.

Understanding Self-Care
Self-care refers to the practices and activities that individuals engage in to nurture their physical, mental, and emotional well-being. For someone with narcissistic traits, self-care can sometimes be misconstrued as self-indulgence or a pursuit of personal gratification at the expense of others. However, true self-care is about recognizing one's needs and boundaries and understanding that taking care of oneself is fundamental to being able to care for others effectively.

Effective self-care might include activities such as:

- **Setting Boundaries:** Knowing when to say no and protecting your time and energy is a vital component of healthy self-care. This means understanding your limits and ensuring that you are not overextending yourself to meet the demands of others.

- **Engaging in Healthy Activities:** Pursuing hobbies, exercising, and spending time in nature are all ways to recharge and reconnect with oneself. These activities can help individuals gain perspective and improve their emotional resilience.

- **Seeking Support:** Whether through therapy, support groups, or trusted friends, seeking help is a crucial form of self-care. It provides a space for reflection and growth, allowing individuals to process their feelings and experiences.

The Role of Responsibility in Relationships

Responsibility in relationships involves recognizing one's role and contributions to the dynamics of the relationship. This includes being accountable for one's actions, being available to support loved ones, and contributing positively to the relationship's health. Individuals with narcissistic traits may struggle with accountability, often deflecting blame or minimizing their impact on others.

Key aspects of responsibility include:

- **Active Listening:** Being present and attentive to the needs and concerns of others is essential. This not only fosters trust but also encourages open communication, which is vital for resolving conflicts and strengthening bonds.

- **Empathy:** Taking the time to understand and validate the feelings of others is crucial. Practicing empathy can help combat self-centered tendencies and promote a more balanced perspective within relationships.

- **Reliability:** Fulfilling commitments and being dependable is a cornerstone of healthy relationships. This shows respect for others' time and emotions, reinforcing the idea that you value the relationship.

Finding the Balance

Finding a harmonious balance between self-care and responsibility is a continuous journey, particularly for those with narcissistic traits. Here are some strategies to help in this endeavor:

1. Self-Assessment: Regularly evaluate your needs and responsibilities. Are you feeling drained or resentful? This may indicate a need to prioritize self-care.

2. Open Dialogue: Communicate with loved ones about your needs and boundaries. Encourage them to express their needs as well, creating an environment of mutual respect and understanding.

3. Mindfulness Practices: Engage in mindfulness or meditation to enhance self-awareness. This can help you identify when you are neglecting self-care or overcommitting to responsibilities.

4. Setting Goals: Establish specific, achievable goals for both self-care and relationship responsibilities. This can provide clarity and direction, helping to maintain a healthy balance.

5. Regular Reflection: At the end of each week, take time to reflect on your self-care practices and your responsibilities. Assess what worked, what didn't, and how you can adjust moving forward.

In conclusion, balancing self-care and responsibility in relationships is crucial for fostering healthy connections and personal growth. By prioritizing both aspects, individuals can cultivate more meaningful, empathetic, and fulfilling relationships while also nurturing their own well-being. This balance not only enriches one's life but also enhances the quality of interactions with others, paving the way for deeper understanding and connection.

Chapter 11

Narcissism in the Workplace

How Narcissism Manifests in Professional Settings

Narcissism, characterized by an inflated sense of self-importance, a deep need for admiration, and a lack of empathy, can significantly impact professional environments. Understanding how narcissistic tendencies manifest in the workplace is crucial for fostering healthy team dynamics and maintaining a positive organizational culture.

1. Leadership Styles:

Narcissism often shapes leadership behaviors, leading to a distinctive style that can be both alluring and detrimental. Narcissistic leaders may present themselves charismatically, using their charm to attract followers and gain admiration. Their confidence can initially inspire teams; however, this often masks an underlying self-serving agenda. Such leaders might prioritize personal accolades over team success, fostering a culture where individual achievements are celebrated at the expense of collaborative efforts. As a result, team members may feel undervalued, leading to decreased morale and increased turnover.

2. Communication Patterns:

In professional settings, narcissists typically exhibit specific communication styles that can be disruptive. They may dominate conversations, steering discussions toward their own ideas or experiences, thus stifling input from others. This monopolization can lead to feelings of frustration among colleagues, who may feel sidelined or unappreciated. Additionally, narcissists may react defensively to constructive criticism, interpreting feedback as personal attacks. This reactivity can create a hostile work environment, discouraging open dialogue and collaboration.

3. Team Dynamics:

Narcissistic individuals often struggle with empathy, which can hinder team dynamics. They may fail to recognize or appreciate the contributions of others, leading to resentment among team members. This lack of recognition can create a toxic atmosphere where individuals feel compelled to compete for the attention and validation of the narcissistic colleague. Such competition often undermines teamwork, as collaborative efforts are overshadowed by personal ambitions.

4. Conflict Management:
A narcissistic approach to conflict can escalate tensions within the workplace. When faced with disagreements, narcissists may resort to manipulation, blame-shifting, or aggression rather than seeking resolution. Their tendency to dismiss others' perspectives can lead to unresolved issues that fester and grow, further complicating relationships within the team. This adversarial approach not only impacts the individuals involved but can also create a wider culture of distrust and fear.

5. Impact on Employee Well-Being
The presence of narcissism in professional settings can have detrimental effects on employee well-being. Individuals working under narcissistic leaders may experience increased stress, anxiety, and burnout due to the constant pressure to meet unrealistic expectations or to seek approval. This toxic environment can lead to decreased job satisfaction, lower productivity, and even physical health issues. Over time, employees may choose to disengage or leave the organization altogether, resulting in high turnover rates.

6. Cultivating Empathy and Respect:
To mitigate the negative effects of narcissism in the workplace, organizations can implement strategies to promote empathy and respect among employees. Training programs focused on emotional intelligence, conflict resolution, and effective communication can foster a culture of understanding and collaboration. Encouraging feedback and open dialogue can empower employees to voice their concerns and contribute to a more inclusive environment.

In conclusion, narcissism presents unique challenges in professional settings, impacting leadership, communication, team dynamics, conflict resolution, and employee well-being. Recognizing these patterns is the first step toward addressing them effectively, paving the way for healthier, more productive workplace relationships. Organizations that prioritize empathy, respect, and open communication can create an environment where all employees feel valued and motivated to contribute to collective success.

Managing Power and Authority Without Narcissism
In today's fast-paced and competitive work environment, the ability to manage power and authority without succumbing to narcissistic tendencies is pivotal for fostering a healthy organizational culture. Narcissism, characterized by grandiosity, entitlement, and a lack of empathy, can distort leadership and undermine team dynamics. Thus, cultivating a leadership style that is both effective and devoid of narcissistic traits is crucial for sustainable success and employee well-being.

Understanding Power Dynamic
To manage power effectively, leaders must first understand the dynamics of power and authority within their organization. Power can be derived from various sources, including position, expertise, and interpersonal relationships. However, wielding power responsibly means recognizing that it is a privilege, not a right. Leaders should strive to empower others rather than exert control over them. This shift in perspective fosters collaboration and trust, which are essential for a healthy workplace environment.

Emphasizing Servant Leadership
One effective approach to managing power without narcissism is through the concept of servant leadership. This model prioritizes the needs of employees and encourages leaders to serve rather than dominate. By focusing on the growth and well-being of team members, leaders can cultivate an inclusive atmosphere where everyone feels valued. Servant leaders actively listen, provide support, and encourage professional development, which can lead to higher morale and productivity.

Practicing Empathy and Emotional Intelligence
Empathy is a critical component of effective leadership. Leaders who understand and relate to the emotions of their team members are better equipped to manage their authority without resorting to narcissistic behaviors. Developing emotional intelligence involves being aware of one's own emotions and those of others, which can help to navigate difficult conversations and conflicts. By practicing empathy, leaders can foster a sense of belonging and community within their teams, reducing feelings of alienation or resentment that often accompany hierarchical structures.

Setting Healthy Boundaries
A healthy approach to managing power also includes establishing clear boundaries. Leaders must communicate expectations and limitations while respecting the autonomy of their team members. This balance prevents overreach and fosters an environment where employees feel safe to express their ideas and concerns. Setting boundaries is not only about maintaining authority; it's also about creating a culture of respect and accountability. When leaders model healthy boundaries, they encourage their teams to do the same, which can lead to improved relationships and a more cohesive work environment.

Encouraging Open Communication
Open lines of communication are essential for mitigating the risks associated with power and authority. Leaders should create a culture where feedback is not only welcomed but encouraged. By fostering an environment where employees can voice their opinions without fear of

retaliation, leaders can reduce the likelihood of narcissistic behaviors taking root. Encouraging regular check-ins and team meetings allows for transparency and collaboration, enabling everyone to feel heard and valued.

Leading by Example
Ultimately, a leader's behavior sets the tone for the entire organization. By embodying humility, accountability, and respect, leaders can inspire their teams to adopt similar values. This not only helps to diminish narcissistic tendencies but also cultivates a culture of ethical leadership. Leaders should be willing to admit mistakes, express vulnerability, and demonstrate gratitude for their team's contributions. Such practices reinforce the idea that leadership is a shared responsibility, not a platform for personal aggrandizement.

In conclusion, managing power and authority without narcissism is a multifaceted endeavor that requires self-awareness, empathy, and a commitment to serving others. By adopting a servant leadership approach, practicing emotional intelligence, setting healthy boundaries, encouraging open communication, and leading by example, leaders can create a positive organizational culture that promotes collaboration and mutual respect. In doing so, they not only enhance their effectiveness as leaders but also contribute to the overall well-being and success of their teams.

Collaborative Work vs. Self-Centered Leadership
In an era where teamwork and collaboration are often heralded as the keys to success, understanding the dynamics between collaborative work and self-centered leadership is crucial. At the heart of this discussion lies the contrasting approaches to leadership and team dynamics, particularly in how they influence workplace culture, productivity, and employee morale.

Self-Centered Leadership Defined
Self-centered leadership is characterized by leaders who prioritize their own needs, ambitions, and recognition over those of their team members and the organization as a whole. This leadership style often manifests in various detrimental behaviors, such as micromanagement, a lack of transparency, and an unwillingness to share credit for successes. Self-centered leaders frequently seek admiration and validation, which can lead to a toxic workplace environment where employees feel undervalued and demotivated. The implications of this leadership style can be extensive; it can stifle creativity, inhibit open communication, and foster a culture of fear and competition rather than collaboration.

The Essence of Collaborative Work
In contrast, collaborative work emphasizes teamwork, open communication, and shared goals. Leaders who embody collaborative principles cultivate an inclusive environment where every

team member feels valued and empowered to contribute their unique skills and perspectives. This approach encourages collective problem-solving, promotes creative thinking, and ultimately leads to higher job satisfaction and retention. Collaborative leaders actively seek input from their teams, recognize individual contributions, and celebrate successes as a group, thereby fostering a sense of belonging and purpose among team members.

The Impact of Leadership Styles on Team Dynamics

The leadership style adopted by an organization can significantly influence team dynamics. In self-centered leadership scenarios, team members may become disengaged, leading to a drop in morale. This disengagement often manifests as reduced productivity, increased absenteeism, and a higher turnover rate. Employees may feel compelled to compete against one another rather than collaborate, resulting in a fragmented team that struggles to achieve common goals.

Conversely, collaborative work environments enhance team cohesion and collective efficacy. When leaders prioritize collaboration, they create a safe space for team members to express ideas, share feedback, and support one another. This nurturing atmosphere fosters trust and respect, which are essential for effective teamwork. As team members feel appreciated and understood, their commitment to shared objectives strengthens, leading to superior performance and innovation.

Navigating the Shift from Self-Centered to Collaborative Leadership

Transitioning from self-centered leadership to a more collaborative approach requires intentional effort and self-awareness. Leaders must recognize their own tendencies towards narcissistic behaviors and actively work to mitigate them. This can involve seeking feedback from team members, engaging in self-reflection, and committing to personal growth.

Practices such as active listening, empathy training, and developing emotional intelligence can significantly enhance a leader's capacity to foster collaboration. Additionally, establishing a culture of accountability and transparency is vital. Leaders can model collaborative behaviors by encouraging open discussions, soliciting diverse viewpoints, and recognizing the contributions of all team members.

Conclusion

In summary, the dichotomy between collaborative work and self-centered leadership is stark and impactful. Organizations led by self-centered leaders often face challenges related to employee engagement and productivity, while those that embrace collaborative principles can unlock the full potential of their teams. By cultivating a collaborative leadership style, leaders not only enhance their own effectiveness but also contribute to a healthier, more dynamic workplace that values each individual's contributions. Ultimately, the shift towards collaboration not only benefits the organization but also fosters a culture of mutual respect and shared success, creating a more fulfilling work environment for everyone involved.

How Narcissism Affects Team Dynamics

Narcissism, characterized by grandiosity, a strong need for admiration, and a lack of empathy, can significantly impact team dynamics in workplace settings. Understanding these effects is crucial for fostering a collaborative and productive work environment. When individuals with narcissistic traits are part of a team, their behaviors can lead to both overt and subtle disruptions.

1. Disruption of Collaboration:

Narcissistic individuals often prioritize their own needs and ambitions over the collective goals of the team. This self-centeredness can manifest in various ways, such as dominating conversations, dismissing the ideas of others, or undermining colleagues' contributions. Their need for admiration may drive them to seek the spotlight, stifling collaboration and discouraging team members from sharing their insights or taking initiative. Consequently, the overall team creativity and problem-solving abilities may diminish, as collaborative dialogue becomes overshadowed by the narcissist's desire for validation.

2. Erosion of Trust:

Trust is a foundational element of effective teamwork. However, narcissistic individuals are often perceived as manipulative or insincere, which can erode trust within the team. Their tendency to engage in blame-shifting and a lack of accountability can create an environment of suspicion. Team members may hesitate to rely on a narcissistic colleague or to express their vulnerabilities, fearing that their contributions will be belittled or exploited. This atmosphere can lead to psychological disengagement, where team members become less motivated to collaborate and support one another.

3. Conflict and Tension:

Narcissism can also escalate conflict within teams. Individuals with narcissistic traits may struggle with accepting feedback and criticism, viewing it as a personal attack rather than an opportunity for growth. This defensiveness can lead to frequent disagreements, as they might respond with hostility or passive-aggressive behaviors when confronted. The resulting tension can create a toxic work environment, where team members feel uncomfortable expressing differing opinions or addressing issues directly.

4. Impact on Leadership:
Narcissistic leaders can pose unique challenges for team dynamics. While they may initially appear charismatic and inspiring, their leadership style often lacks the essential qualities of empathy and support. Narcissistic leaders tend to make decisions based on personal gain rather than the best interest of the team. This can lead to favoritism, where certain team members are given preferential treatment, further fracturing team cohesion. Their focus on personal achievements can overshadow team accomplishments, diminishing collective morale.

5. Performance and Productivity:
The presence of narcissism in a team can ultimately hinder overall performance and productivity. As team members become disengaged or demoralized due to the disruptive behaviors of a narcissistic individual, the quality of work may decline. Creativity and innovation may stagnate, as individuals may be less willing to take risks or share ideas in an environment that does not foster mutual respect and support.

6. Developing Healthy Team Dynamics:
To mitigate the impact of narcissism on team dynamics, organizations can adopt strategies that promote a culture of openness and collaboration. Establishing clear communication protocols, encouraging constructive feedback, and fostering an atmosphere of psychological safety can help counteract the negative effects of narcissism. Leadership training focused on emotional intelligence and empathy can also equip leaders with the tools necessary to manage narcissistic traits effectively.

In conclusion, while narcissism can pose significant challenges to team dynamics, recognizing its effects and implementing proactive strategies can help organizations create healthier, more productive work environments. By fostering collaboration, trust, and accountability, teams can navigate the complexities introduced by narcissism, ultimately enhancing their collective performance and well-being.

Cultivating Empathy and Respect in Professional Relationships
In today's fast-paced work environments, the significance of empathy and respect cannot be overstated. Healthy professional relationships are built on these foundational elements, which not only foster collaboration but also enhance overall workplace morale and productivity. Cultivating empathy and respect requires intentional effort and consistent practice. Here are key strategies for embedding these values into the workplace.

Understanding Empathy in Professional Contexts
Empathy is the ability to understand and share the feelings of another. In the workplace, it

allows colleagues to connect on a human level, facilitating better communication and teamwork. There are two main types of empathy relevant to professional settings: cognitive empathy, which involves understanding another's perspective, and emotional empathy, which involves feeling what another person feels. Both forms are essential in recognizing and validating the experiences of others, leading to stronger interpersonal connections.

Active Listening: The Cornerstone of Empathy

Active listening is a critical skill for cultivating empathy and respect. It involves fully concentrating on what is being said, rather than just passively hearing the message. This requires setting aside distractions, maintaining eye contact, and providing feedback that shows understanding. By engaging in active listening, employees can create a safe space for open dialogue, where colleagues feel valued and heard. This practice not only strengthens relationships but also enhances problem-solving capabilities, as team members are more likely to share ideas and concerns when they feel respected.

Encouraging Open Communication

Creating an environment that encourages open communication is vital for fostering empathy and respect. This can be achieved by promoting a culture where feedback is welcomed and mistakes are viewed as learning opportunities. When team members feel comfortable expressing themselves without fear of judgment, it leads to more authentic interactions and a greater willingness to collaborate. Leaders play a crucial role in modeling this behavior by actively seeking input from their teams and demonstrating vulnerability.

Building Emotional Intelligence

Emotional intelligence (EI) encompasses the ability to recognize, understand, and manage our own emotions while also being attuned to the emotions of others. Developing EI can significantly enhance the ability to empathize. Professional development programs that focus on emotional intelligence training can equip employees with the skills to navigate complex interpersonal dynamics. Through increased self-awareness and social awareness, individuals can better respond to the emotional needs of their colleagues, thus fostering a more respectful and empathetic work environment.

Practicing Perspective-Taking

Perspective-taking is a powerful tool for enhancing empathy in professional relationships. Encouraging team members to consider situations from different viewpoints can lead to greater understanding and respect for diverse opinions and backgrounds. This can be facilitated through team-building activities that promote collaboration and shared experiences. When employees engage in exercises that require them to step into each other's shoes, they gain insights that foster mutual respect and empathy.

Recognizing and Respecting Diversity
Workplaces today are often characterized by diverse teams, bringing varied perspectives shaped by different backgrounds, cultures, and life experiences. Recognizing and respecting this diversity is crucial for cultivating empathy. Organizations can promote inclusivity by implementing diversity training and creating policies that celebrate differences. By valuing each individual's unique contributions, teams can build a culture of respect that enhances collaboration and innovation.

Conclusion
Cultivating empathy and respect in professional relationships is an ongoing journey that requires commitment from all team members. By prioritizing active listening, open communication, emotional intelligence, perspective-taking, and diversity, organizations can create a supportive environment where empathy thrives. As team members practice these skills, they not only enhance their relationships with one another but also contribute to a more positive and productive workplace culture. In doing so, they pave the way for improved teamwork, creativity, and overall job satisfaction, leading to lasting professional success.

Chapter 12

Dealing with Narcissism in Others

Recognizing Narcissistic Traits in Others

Narcissism, a personality trait characterized by an inflated sense of self-importance, a deep need for admiration, and a lack of empathy, can manifest in various ways in interpersonal relationships. Understanding how to recognize narcissistic traits in others is crucial for maintaining healthy boundaries and fostering emotional well-being. This section will explore key indicators of narcissism, helping individuals identify these behaviors in their relationships with friends, family members, colleagues, or acquaintances.

1. Grandiosity and Self-Importance:
One of the hallmark traits of narcissism is grandiosity. Narcissistic individuals often exhibit an exaggerated sense of their own abilities, achievements, and importance. They may boast about their accomplishments or seek to elevate themselves in conversations, often disregarding the contributions or feelings of others. Statements that reflect a sense of superiority, such as "I'm the best at what I do" or "People depend on me more than anyone else," are common.

2. Need for Admiration:
Narcissists have a constant craving for admiration and validation from others. They may fish for compliments or become visibly upset if they feel overlooked or undervalued. Their conversations often center around themselves, and they may struggle to engage in genuine dialogue that includes the perspectives or experiences of others. If you find someone frequently seeking attention or praise, it may indicate narcissistic tendencies.

3. Lack of Empathy:
A significant characteristic of narcissism is the inability or unwillingness to empathize with others. Narcissistic individuals may dismiss or belittle the emotions and experiences of those around them. For instance, if a friend shares a difficult experience and the response is a shift back to their own issues or a lack of acknowledgment, this could be a sign of narcissistic traits.

4. Manipulative Behavior:
Narcissists often use manipulation as a tool to get what they want. This can manifest as guilt-tripping, gaslighting, or other forms of emotional manipulation to maintain control in relationships. You might notice that certain individuals often twist facts or narratives to portray themselves as victims, thereby diverting attention from their own shortcomings and placing

blame on others.

5. Entitlement:
A sense of entitlement is another common trait among narcissistic individuals. They may believe that they deserve special treatment or that rules do not apply to them. This can manifest in various contexts, such as expecting preferential treatment at work or in social settings, or being dismissive of others' needs and feelings. If someone consistently acts as though they are above others, it may be a sign of narcissism.

6. Fragile Self-Esteem:
Although narcissists appear confident, their self-esteem is often fragile. They may react defensively to criticism or perceived slights, displaying anger, contempt, or even withdrawal. This volatility can create a tense atmosphere in relationships, as their reactions may seem disproportionate to the situation. If someone tends to lash out or sulk excessively when faced with constructive feedback, they may exhibit narcissistic traits.

7. Exploitative Relationships:
Narcissists often form relationships that serve their interests, using others as tools for their own gain. They may lack genuine interest in others' well-being unless it benefits them. If you notice a pattern of one-sided relationships, where the narcissistic individual consistently prioritizes their needs above those of others, it could signal a narcissistic personality.

Conclusion:
Recognizing narcissistic traits in others is essential for safeguarding emotional health and establishing healthy boundaries. By being aware of behaviors such as grandiosity, a need for admiration, lack of empathy, manipulative tactics, entitlement, fragile self-esteem, and exploitative relationships, individuals can make informed decisions about their interactions. Understanding these signs not only aids in personal relationships but also promotes a more empathetic and supportive social environment.

Setting Boundaries with Narcissistic People
Establishing boundaries with narcissistic individuals is a crucial skill for maintaining your emotional well-being and protecting your personal space. Narcissism often manifests as self-centeredness, entitlement, and a lack of empathy, which can lead to toxic dynamics in relationships. This section provides practical strategies for setting and maintaining healthy boundaries when dealing with narcissistic people.

Understanding Boundaries
Boundaries are personal guidelines that define how you wish to be treated by others. They serve to protect your emotional and physical space and help establish clear expectations within relationships. In interactions with narcissistic individuals, boundaries become particularly essential. Such individuals often disregard others' feelings and needs, making it vital to assert your own limits firmly.

Identifying Your Needs
The first step in setting boundaries is identifying your own needs and limits. Reflect on the behaviors that make you uncomfortable or distressed. It may involve recognizing when a narcissistic person is monopolizing conversations, dismissing your feelings, or demanding more time and energy than you can give. Understanding your triggers will empower you to articulate your boundaries clearly.

Communicating Boundaries Clearly
Once you've identified your needs, communicate them directly and assertively. Use "I" statements to express your feelings and needs without sounding accusatory. For example, instead of saying, "You always interrupt me," you might say, "I feel unheard when conversations are dominated. I need some time to share my thoughts." This approach minimizes defensiveness and emphasizes your experience rather than placing blame.

Be Consistent
Consistency is key when enforcing boundaries with narcissistic individuals. They may test your limits repeatedly, seeking to revert to familiar patterns of behavior. It is crucial to remain steadfast in your boundaries. If you've established that you will not engage in conversations that belittle or ignore you, stick to that decision. Inconsistency can lead to confusion and reinforce their disregard for your limits.

Expect Pushback
Narcissistic individuals may react negatively when confronted with boundaries. They might employ tactics such as guilt-tripping, manipulation, or anger to regain control. It's essential to remain calm and resolute. Understand that their reactions are reflections of their own issues, not a failure on your part to set healthy boundaries. Prepare yourself mentally for these responses and remind yourself of the importance of maintaining your limits.

Practice Self-Care
Setting boundaries can be emotionally taxing, especially when dealing with a narcissistic person. Incorporate self-care practices into your routine to support your mental health. Engage

in activities that restore your energy and help you process your emotions, such as mindfulness, exercise, journaling, or spending time with supportive friends. Prioritizing self-care reinforces your commitment to your boundaries and enhances your emotional resilience.

Know When to Walk Away
In some cases, despite your best efforts, a narcissistic individual may refuse to respect your boundaries. It's essential to recognize when a relationship is detrimental to your mental health. If attempts to set boundaries lead to increased conflict or emotional distress, it may be necessary to distance yourself from that person. Walking away from toxic relationships can be a powerful act of self-preservation and a crucial step towards emotional healing.

Conclusion
Setting boundaries with narcissistic people is essential for maintaining your well-being and fostering healthier interactions. By identifying your needs, communicating them clearly, remaining consistent, and practicing self-care, you can protect yourself from the potential emotional harm associated with narcissistic behaviors. Remember, it's not just about establishing limits; it's about reclaiming your space and promoting a more balanced, respectful relationship dynamic.

Navigating Conflict with Narcissistic Individuals
Conflict with narcissistic individuals can be particularly challenging due to their characteristic traits such as a lack of empathy, a need for control, and a propensity for manipulation. Navigating such conflicts requires a nuanced approach that prioritizes your well-being while aiming for a constructive resolution. Below are strategies to effectively manage and resolve conflicts with narcissistic individuals.

Understanding the Narcissistic Mindset
Before engaging in conflict, it's essential to recognize the mindset of a narcissistic individual. They often view situations in black-and-white terms, see themselves as superior, and may react defensively to perceived slights or criticism. Their responses can be unpredictable, ranging from anger and blame to passive-aggressive behaviors. Understanding this context can help you prepare mentally and emotionally for the interaction.

Maintain Emotional Detachment
One of the most effective strategies when navigating conflict with narcissistic individuals is to maintain emotional detachment. This does not mean being cold or dismissive, but rather guarding your emotional state against their manipulative tactics. They may provoke emotional reactions to gain control or shift the narrative. By staying composed and responding in a calm

manner, you can minimize the chances of escalating the conflict.

Use Clear and Direct Communication
When addressing issues with a narcissistic individual, clarity is key. Use direct, assertive communication without resorting to emotional language or accusations. For example, instead of saying, "You never listen to me," you might say, "I feel unheard when you interrupt me during discussions." This approach reduces defensiveness and centers the conversation on specific behaviors rather than personal attacks.

Set Boundaries
Establishing and maintaining boundaries is crucial in any relationship, particularly with narcissistic individuals. Clearly define what behaviors are acceptable and what are not, and communicate these boundaries firmly. For instance, if the individual often raises their voice during disagreements, you might state, "I am willing to discuss this, but I need you to speak to me respectfully." Be prepared to enforce these boundaries consistently, as narcissistic individuals may test limits.

Focus on Solutions
During conflicts, narcissists may become fixated on winning or being right rather than resolving the issue. To counteract this, steer the conversation toward solutions. Ask open-ended questions like, "What can we do to resolve this?" or "How can we move forward?" This shifts the focus from blame to collaboration, making it easier for both parties to find common ground.

Prepare for Resistance
Narcissistic individuals may resist compromise or refuse to acknowledge their role in conflicts. This resistance can lead to prolonged discussions and increased frustration. Prepare yourself for this possibility by having a plan in place. If the conversation becomes unproductive, consider taking a break and revisiting the issue later. You might say, "I think it's best if we pause this discussion and come back to it when we're both calmer."

Prioritize Self-Care
Finally, navigating conflict with narcissistic individuals can be emotionally exhausting. Prioritize self-care before and after these interactions by engaging in activities that rejuvenate you, such as exercise, meditation, or spending time with supportive friends. Reflect on the conversation and your feelings afterward to process any emotional turmoil. This practice not only helps in healing but also builds resilience for future interactions.

Conclusion
Navigating conflict with narcissistic individuals is undoubtedly complex and often fraught with emotional challenges. By employing strategies such as maintaining emotional detachment, communicating clearly, setting firm boundaries, and focusing on solutions, you can manage these interactions more effectively. Remember, your emotional health is paramount, and taking steps to protect it while seeking resolution is a powerful act of self-care.

Protecting Your Self-Esteem and Well-Being
Self-esteem is a crucial component of mental health, influencing how we view ourselves and interact with others. For individuals dealing with the effects of narcissism, whether in themselves or in relationships with narcissistic individuals, safeguarding self-esteem becomes vital. This section explores strategies to protect your self-esteem and overall well-being, focusing on awareness, boundaries, and positive self-affirmation.

Understanding Self-Esteem
Self-esteem refers to the subjective evaluation of one's worth and value. It is shaped by experiences, relationships, and internal dialogues. Healthy self-esteem allows individuals to face life's challenges with resilience, while low self-esteem can lead to feelings of inadequacy, anxiety, and depression. When entangled with narcissistic dynamics, self-esteem can be severely compromised, resulting in a cycle of validation-seeking, emotional pain, and unhealthy relational patterns.

Recognizing the Impact of Narcissism
In relationships with narcissistic individuals, self-esteem can take a hit through manipulation, gaslighting, and emotional abuse. Narcissists often project their insecurities onto others, creating an environment where self-worth becomes contingent upon their approval. Recognizing these dynamics is the first step in protecting your self-esteem. Awareness allows individuals to identify harmful behaviors, set boundaries, and begin the healing process.

Establishing Healthy Boundaries
Boundaries are essential for maintaining self-esteem and well-being. They define where one person ends and another begins, helping to protect personal space, emotional health, and self-worth. Here are key aspects of establishing healthy boundaries:

1. Know Your Limits: Understand what behaviors are unacceptable to you. This may involve reflecting on past experiences to identify patterns that have harmed your self-esteem.

2. Communicate Clearly: Once you identify your limits, communicate them assertively to those around you. Use "I" statements to express your feelings without assigning blame, such as, "I feel uncomfortable when you criticize my choices."

3. Be Consistent: Enforcing boundaries consistently is crucial. If a boundary is crossed, address it immediately. Consistency reinforces your self-worth and signals to others that you value yourself.

4. Practice Saying No: It's okay to prioritize your well-being. Saying no to requests that drain your energy or compromise your values is essential for maintaining healthy self-esteem.

Cultivating Positive Self-Affirmation

Affirmations are powerful tools for enhancing self-esteem. They can counter negative self-talk often exacerbated by interactions with narcissistic individuals. Here are ways to cultivate positive self-affirmation:

1. Daily Affirmations: Create a list of affirmations that resonate with you. These could include statements like, "I am worthy of love and respect" or "I have the strength to face challenges." Repeating these daily can help shift your mindset.

2. Focus on Strengths: Regularly remind yourself of your strengths and achievements. Keeping a journal where you note daily accomplishments, no matter how small, can reinforce a positive self-image.

3. Engage in Self-Care: Prioritize activities that nourish your mind and body. Whether through exercise, hobbies, or relaxation techniques, self-care reinforces self-worth and contributes to emotional resilience.

4. Seek Support: Surround yourself with positive influences. Engage with friends, family, or support groups who uplift you and affirm your value. Their support can help counteract negative messages you may receive from narcissistic individuals.

Conclusion

Protecting your self-esteem and well-being in the context of narcissism requires awareness, boundary-setting, and positive self-affirmation. By recognizing the impact of narcissistic behaviors, establishing firm boundaries, and cultivating positive self-talk, individuals can reclaim their sense of self-worth. This proactive approach not only fosters resilience but also paves the way for healthier relationships and a more fulfilling life. In the journey toward healing, remember that self-esteem is not solely determined by external validation but is inherently rooted in the recognition of your own worth and contributions to the world.

When to Walk Away from Narcissistic Relationships

Navigating relationships with narcissistic individuals can be profoundly challenging and emotionally draining. At some point, recognizing when to walk away becomes crucial for your mental health and overall well-being. Understanding the signs and implications of remaining in such relationships can help you make an informed decision about your future.

Recognizing the Signs

The first step in determining whether to part ways with a narcissistic individual involves recognizing the pervasive patterns of behavior characteristic of narcissism. Narcissistic individuals often exhibit traits such as entitlement, lack of empathy, manipulation, and a constant need for admiration. These behaviors can manifest in various ways, including:

1. Emotional Manipulation: Narcissists often use guilt or manipulation to control others, making you feel responsible for their emotions or well-being.

2. Gaslighting: This psychological manipulation can leave you doubting your perceptions and reality, leading to confusion and self-doubt.

3. Consistent Disregard for Your Needs: In a healthy relationship, mutual respect and consideration are paramount. If your needs are consistently overlooked, it's a significant red flag.

4. Chronic Criticism and Devaluation: Narcissists may alternate between idealizing you and then devaluing you, leading to emotional whiplash and a pervasive sense of inadequacy.

Assessing the Impact on Your Life

Once you've identified narcissistic behaviors, it's essential to evaluate how the relationship affects your mental and emotional health. **Ask yourself the following questions:**

- **Do I feel drained or anxious after interactions?** The emotional toll of dealing with a narcissistic individual can lead to chronic stress and anxiety.

- **Am I losing my sense of self?** Narcissistic relationships often lead to a diminished sense of identity, as your thoughts, feelings, and needs take a backseat to the narcissist's demands.

- Is the relationship one-sided? Healthy relationships are reciprocal. If you find yourself constantly giving without receiving, it may be time to reconsider your involvement.

Setting Boundaries and Communicating

Before making the decision to walk away, attempt to set clear boundaries. Communicate your needs and limits transparently. However, be prepared for potential backlash. Narcissists often resist boundaries, viewing them as threats to their control. If your attempts to establish boundaries are met with hostility or manipulation, this is a strong indicator that the relationship may not be salvageable.

The Decision to Walk Away

Deciding to end a relationship with a narcissistic individual is rarely easy. It can involve feelings of guilt, fear of abandonment, or uncertainty about the future. However, prioritizing your mental health and emotional well-being is paramount. Here are some considerations to help you through this difficult process:

1. Seek Support: Surround yourself with supportive friends, family, or professionals who can provide validation and encouragement during this challenging time.

2. Establish a Safety Plan: If the relationship has involved emotional or physical abuse, ensure you have a safety plan in place before taking any action to leave.

3. Focus on Self-Care: Engage in activities that promote your well-being, reduce stress, and help you reconnect with your sense of self.

4. Prepare for Emotional Aftermath: After ending the relationship, you may experience a range of emotions, including relief, sadness, or even regret. Allow yourself to grieve the loss of the relationship while recognizing it was necessary for your growth.

5. Consider Professional Help: Therapy can provide invaluable support as you navigate the complexities of leaving a narcissistic relationship and rebuilding your life.

Walking away from a narcissistic relationship is not only a courageous act but also a necessary step towards reclaiming your life, fostering self-worth, and cultivating healthier, more fulfilling connections. By recognizing the signs, assessing the impact, and prioritizing your well-being, you can embark on a journey of healing and personal transformation, free from the constraints of narcissistic dynamics.

Chapter 13

Self-Compassion vs. Narcissism

The Difference Between Healthy Self-Love and Narcissism
Self-love and narcissism are often conflated, yet they represent fundamentally different approaches to self-perception and interpersonal relationships. Understanding the distinction between these two concepts is crucial for personal development and fostering healthy relationships with others.

Healthy Self-Love: A Foundation for Well-Being
Healthy self-love is characterized by a balanced, realistic appreciation of oneself. It involves recognizing one's worth, embracing imperfections, and nurturing one's emotional and physical well-being. This form of self-love is rooted in self-acceptance and self-compassion, enabling individuals to treat themselves with kindness and respect. Healthy self-love encourages personal growth, self-awareness, and the pursuit of passions and interests.

A person with healthy self-love recognizes their strengths and accomplishments but does not feel the need to overshadow others or seek validation through comparison. Instead, they find joy in their achievements while also celebrating the successes of those around them. This balanced perspective allows for gratitude and an appreciation of life, promoting resilience in the face of challenges.

Narcissism: An Excessive Focus on Self
In contrast, narcissism is marked by an inflated sense of self-importance and a pervasive need for admiration and validation from others. Individuals exhibiting narcissistic traits often have a distorted self-image that requires constant reinforcement through external accolades and recognition. This need for validation can lead to a preoccupation with one's status, appearance, or accomplishments, often at the expense of empathy and genuine connections with others.

Narcissism often manifests in a lack of regard for the feelings and needs of others. While someone with healthy self-love can empathize and engage in authentic relationships, a narcissistic individual may struggle to recognize or care about the emotions of those around them. This disconnect can result in toxic relationships, where the narcissist's needs overshadow the well-being of others, leading to manipulation or exploitation.

Key Differences: Validation vs. Acceptance

One of the primary differences between healthy self-love and narcissism lies in the source of self-worth. Healthy self-love is internally driven, stemming from self-acceptance and personal values. Individuals who practice self-love derive satisfaction from their intrinsic qualities and the relationships they cultivate. On the other hand, narcissistic individuals seek external validation as a way to affirm their worth. This reliance on external sources creates vulnerability, as their self-esteem fluctuates based on others' opinions or perceptions.

The Role of Empathy

Empathy is another distinguishing factor between self-love and narcissism. Healthy self-love fosters empathy, allowing individuals to connect authentically with others. They can appreciate different perspectives and emotions, which enriches their relationships. Conversely, narcissism often leads to an empathy deficit, where the individual struggles to understand or relate to others' experiences, focusing instead on their own needs and desires.

Cultivating Healthy Self-Love

To cultivate healthy self-love, individuals can engage in practices that promote self-acceptance and emotional well-being. This includes:

1. Self-Reflection: Regularly assessing one's thoughts and feelings can help identify areas for growth and self-improvement without harsh self-judgment.

2. Mindfulness: Practicing mindfulness encourages awareness of the present moment, allowing individuals to appreciate themselves without comparison to others.

3. Setting Boundaries: Healthy self-love involves respecting one's needs and limits, fostering relationships based on mutual respect and empathy.

4. Gratitude Practices: Focusing on gratitude can shift attention from self-centeredness to appreciation for the world and its connections.

In conclusion, while self-love is essential for personal growth and fulfillment, narcissism can lead to destructive patterns that undermine relationships and emotional health. By fostering healthy self-love grounded in acceptance, empathy, and mutual respect, individuals can cultivate a more balanced and fulfilling life.

Practicing Self-Compassion While Avoiding Narcissism

Self-compassion is a vital component of emotional health and well-being, especially for individuals grappling with narcissistic tendencies. It involves treating oneself with kindness, understanding, and acceptance, particularly in times of struggle or failure. However, the challenge lies in distinguishing self-compassion from narcissism, as both concepts can superficially resemble each other, particularly in their focus on the self.

At its core, self-compassion is about recognizing one's humanity and imperfection. It invites individuals to embrace their flaws and mistakes without harsh self-judgment. This practice can alleviate feelings of shame and inadequacy often associated with narcissism. Narcissism typically manifests as an inflated sense of self-importance, often accompanied by a deep-seated need for external validation and an inability to accept flaws. In contrast, self-compassion fosters a balanced self-view that acknowledges both strengths and weaknesses, allowing for growth and learning without the need for constant admiration.

To practice self-compassion without slipping into narcissism, individuals can follow several guiding principles:

1. Mindfulness: Cultivating mindfulness is the first step in developing self-compassion. Mindfulness involves being present in the moment and acknowledging thoughts and feelings without judgment. When individuals become aware of their inner dialogue, they can identify self-critical thoughts that may lead to narcissistic behaviors. By observing these thoughts without attachment, they can create space for self-compassionate responses. For example, instead of berating oneself for making a mistake, a mindful approach allows for recognition of the mistake as part of the human experience.

2. Common Humanity: A key aspect of self-compassion is recognizing that suffering and imperfection are universal experiences. Instead of isolating oneself in shame, individuals can remind themselves that everyone makes mistakes and experiences failures. This perspective helps to counteract the narcissistic tendency to view oneself as unique or special to the exclusion of others. By acknowledging shared human experiences, individuals can foster empathy towards themselves and others, reducing the need for self-aggrandizement.

3. Self-Kindness: Practicing self-kindness means treating oneself as one would treat a friend. When faced with failure or disappointment, individuals should focus on comforting themselves rather than resorting to criticism. This shift in approach encourages a nurturing internal dialogue that affirms one's worth independent of achievements or external validation. For instance, when feeling inadequate, instead of thinking, "I'm a failure," a self-compassionate response might be, "It's okay to fail; I can learn from this experience."

4. Setting Realistic Standards: Narcissism often thrives on the pursuit of perfection. To counter this, individuals should set realistic and achievable goals. This approach encourages a focus on personal growth rather than a relentless pursuit of excellence, which can lead to feelings of inadequacy and the need for validation. By celebrating small victories and acknowledging progress, individuals can cultivate a sense of self-worth that is not contingent on being perfect.

5. Gratitude and Service: Incorporating practices of gratitude and service into daily life can also strengthen self-compassion while mitigating narcissistic tendencies. Expressing gratitude shifts the focus from oneself to appreciating others and the world around us. Additionally, engaging in acts of service fosters a sense of connection and empathy, reinforcing the understanding that fulfillment comes from contributing to the well-being of others, rather than seeking validation through self-centered achievements.

In conclusion, practicing self-compassion while avoiding narcissism is a delicate balance that requires self-awareness and intentionality. By cultivating mindfulness, embracing common humanity, practicing self-kindness, setting realistic standards, and integrating gratitude and service into one's life, individuals can foster a healthier relationship with themselves that promotes growth, resilience, and authentic connections with others. This journey towards self-compassion not only enhances personal well-being but also enriches interpersonal relationships, ultimately leading to a more fulfilling and empathetic life.

The Role of Self-Forgiveness in Personal Growth

Self-forgiveness is a crucial aspect of personal growth, particularly for individuals grappling with narcissistic traits or behaviors. It entails the process of acknowledging one's mistakes, accepting responsibility, and allowing oneself the grace to move forward without being tethered by guilt or shame. This introspective journey not only fosters emotional healing but also cultivates a more authentic and compassionate self, essential for overcoming narcissism.

Understanding Self-Forgiveness

At its core, self-forgiveness is about self-acceptance. It involves recognizing that everyone is imperfect and makes mistakes. For those prone to narcissism, which often stems from a fragile self-esteem, the need for external validation can lead to a cycle of self-criticism and denial. Individuals may struggle with feelings of guilt over past actions or behaviors, particularly if they have hurt others. This emotional burden can hinder personal growth, trapping individuals in a state of reactivity and defensiveness.

Self-forgiveness allows individuals to break this cycle. By acknowledging one's shortcomings without judgment, individuals can begin to view their experiences as opportunities for learning rather than sources of shame. This shift in mindset is vital for fostering resilience and emotional health.

The Process of Self-Forgiveness

1. Acknowledgment: The first step toward self-forgiveness is to confront and acknowledge the behavior or decision that led to feelings of guilt or shame. This requires honesty and self-reflection, often facilitated through journaling or therapy. It's essential to articulate what occurred, the impact it had on oneself and others, and why it was detrimental.

2. Responsibility: Taking ownership of one's actions is crucial. This does not mean wallowing in guilt but rather recognizing that while mistakes are part of being human, they also provide valuable lessons. Accepting responsibility allows individuals to understand the consequences of their actions, which is a stepping stone towards personal growth.

3. Compassion: Practicing self-compassion is vital during this process. Individuals must learn to treat themselves with the same kindness and understanding they would extend to a friend in a similar situation. This involves reframing negative self-talk and replacing it with affirmations of self-worth. Techniques such as mindfulness and meditation can help cultivate a compassionate mindset.

4. Letting Go: Once individuals have acknowledged their mistakes and taken responsibility, the next step is to actively work on letting go of the associated guilt and shame. This may involve visualizing the release of negative emotions or creating rituals that symbolize forgiveness. For instance, writing a letter to oneself expressing forgiveness and then safely disposing of it can provide a tangible sense of closure.

5. Commitment to Change: Self-forgiveness is not merely about absolution; it also entails a commitment to change. Individuals should identify actionable steps they can take to avoid repeating the same mistakes. This might include setting personal goals, developing new coping strategies, or seeking professional help. By focusing on growth and improvement, individuals reinforce a positive self-identity that is not defined by past failures.

The Benefits of Self-Forgiveness

Engaging in self-forgiveness can yield profound benefits for personal growth. It fosters emotional resilience, reduces stress, and enhances overall mental health. By alleviating the burden of guilt, individuals can cultivate a more profound sense of empathy towards themselves and others, which is particularly important for those overcoming narcissistic tendencies.

Moreover, self-forgiveness can significantly improve interpersonal relationships. As individuals learn to forgive themselves, they often become better equipped to forgive others, building healthier and more authentic connections. This process not only enhances one's social interactions but also promotes a more fulfilling life grounded in empathy and understanding.

In conclusion, self-forgiveness is an integral component of personal growth, particularly for those struggling with narcissistic traits. By acknowledging past actions, embracing responsibility, and fostering compassion, individuals can pave the way for emotional healing and transformation, ultimately leading to a more authentic and fulfilling life.

Cultivating Self-Worth Without Seeking External Validation

In a world increasingly driven by social media, public approval, and external accolades, the journey toward cultivating self-worth independent of external validation can be both challenging and transformative. To foster a sense of self-worth that is rooted in internal values rather than external perceptions, individuals must engage in intentional practices that promote self-acceptance, self-compassion, and authenticity.

Understanding Self-Worth

Self-worth is the intrinsic value one assigns to oneself, independent of achievements, social status, or the opinions of others. It forms the foundation of a healthy self-image and contributes significantly to emotional well-being. When self-worth is tied to external validation, it becomes fragile and susceptible to fluctuations based on others' opinions or societal standards. By contrast, cultivating self-worth from within allows individuals to build a resilient and stable self-concept.

Strategies for Cultivating Self-Worth

1. Practice Self-Reflection

Self-reflection is a powerful tool for understanding oneself better. Regularly set aside time to reflect on your values, beliefs, and experiences. Journaling can be particularly effective; write about your strengths, accomplishments, and the qualities you appreciate in yourself. This practice helps solidify a positive self-image and reinforces the idea that your worth does not depend on outside approval.

2. Set Personal Goals Aligned with Your Values

Identify what truly matters to you and set goals that reflect your values rather than societal expectations. Focus on personal growth, skill development, or pursuing passions that resonate with your authentic self. Achieving these self-defined goals fosters a sense of accomplishment that is intrinsic and fulfilling.

3. Embrace Self-Compassion

Self-compassion involves treating oneself with the same kindness and understanding that one would offer a friend. Acknowledge that everyone makes mistakes and faces challenges; these experiences do not diminish your worth. Practice self-kindness, recognize your shared humanity, and cultivate mindfulness to avoid self-criticism. This compassionate approach nurtures a positive self-concept and allows you to embrace imperfections.

4. Limit Comparison

Comparison to others can be detrimental to self-worth. In a culture that often promotes competition and envy, it's essential to recognize that everyone has a unique journey. Instead of measuring your worth against others, focus on your personal growth and celebrate your individual achievements. When you catch yourself comparing, consciously redirect your thoughts to gratitude for your own journey.

5. Develop a Growth Mindset

Adopting a growth mindset means viewing challenges as opportunities for learning rather than threats to your self-worth. Embrace failures as part of the growth process and recognize that effort and perseverance lead to improvement. This mindset fosters resilience and allows you to appreciate your progress, reinforcing the belief that your worth is inherent and not contingent on success.

6. Engage in Meaningful Activities

Invest time in activities that bring you joy and fulfillment, whether through hobbies, volunteer work, or creative pursuits. Engaging in meaningful activities fosters a sense of purpose and connects you to your inner self, reinforcing the belief that you are valuable for who you are, not just what you achieve.

7. Build Healthy Relationships

Surround yourself with supportive individuals who appreciate you for your authentic self. Healthy relationships encourage you to express your true identity and reinforce a sense of worth that is independent of external validation. Seek connections that prioritize mutual respect, understanding, and encouragement.

8. Practice Gratitude
Regularly acknowledging the positive aspects of your life can shift your focus from what you lack to what you have. Cultivating gratitude helps reinforce the belief that you are enough as you are. Consider maintaining a gratitude journal, where you note things you appreciate about yourself and your life.

By implementing these strategies, individuals can cultivate self-worth that is resilient, authentic, and fulfilling. This journey requires patience and persistence, but the rewards—greater emotional stability, improved relationships, and a deeper connection to oneself—are well worth the effort. In a society that often equates worth with external accolades, reclaiming and nurturing a self-worth grounded in internal validation is a powerful act of self-empowerment.

Developing a Growth Mindset

A growth mindset, a term popularized by psychologist Carol Dweck, refers to the belief that abilities and intelligence can be developed through dedication, hard work, and resilience. This mindset contrasts sharply with a fixed mindset, which holds that our qualities are static and unchangeable. For individuals grappling with narcissistic tendencies, developing a growth mindset is crucial for personal transformation and rebuilding relationships. It encourages an openness to learning and fosters an environment where self-improvement is not only possible but also celebrated.

Embracing Challenges

One of the fundamental aspects of a growth mindset is the willingness to embrace challenges rather than avoid them. For those struggling with narcissism, challenges often feel threatening and may trigger defensiveness or denial. However, by reframing challenges as opportunities for growth, individuals can begin to shift their perspective. For instance, facing constructive criticism can be viewed as a chance to learn rather than an attack on one's character. Adopting this viewpoint can help to lessen the fear of failure and promote a more resilient approach to personal and professional setbacks.

Learning from Feedback

Incorporating feedback into one's understanding of self is another vital component of a growth mindset. Individuals with narcissistic traits often struggle with accepting criticism, leading to a cycle of defensiveness and avoidance. However, feedback is instrumental in personal growth. It provides insights into our behaviors and can guide us toward healthier interactions with others. Establishing a habit of seeking out constructive feedback from trusted friends, family, or colleagues can help nurture a growth mindset. This practice encourages humility and acknowledgment of one's areas for improvement, facilitating a journey toward greater self-awareness.

Cultivating a Love for Learning
A growth mindset flourishes in an environment that values learning. To cultivate this mindset, individuals should actively seek learning opportunities that challenge their current skills and knowledge. This could involve pursuing new hobbies, engaging in educational workshops, or reading books that expand understanding of emotional intelligence and interpersonal relationships. By prioritizing learning, individuals can shift the focus from self-centeredness to curiosity about the world and the people around them. This shift fosters empathy and enhances one's ability to connect meaningfully with others.

Resilience in the Face of Setbacks
Resilience is a key characteristic of a growth mindset. Developing the ability to bounce back from setbacks and view them as part of the learning process is essential for anyone looking to overcome narcissistic tendencies. Instead of becoming overwhelmed by failures, individuals should practice self-compassion and recognize that setbacks are not a reflection of their worth but rather stepping stones toward growth. Techniques such as journaling can help individuals process their emotions during difficult times, enabling them to reflect on what they've learned and how they can improve moving forward.

Practicing Gratitude and Humility
Gratitude and humility are powerful antidotes to narcissistic tendencies. Individuals can cultivate a growth mindset by regularly practicing gratitude, which shifts the focus away from self-centeredness and towards appreciation for the experiences and people in their lives. Keeping a gratitude journal, where individuals note things they are thankful for each day, can help reinforce this practice. Additionally, embracing humility—recognizing that everyone has strengths and weaknesses—can create a more balanced view of oneself in relation to others. This perspective fosters a sense of connection, reducing the feelings of isolation that often accompany narcissistic traits.

Conclusion
Developing a growth mindset is a transformative journey that can significantly impact individuals struggling with narcissism. By embracing challenges, learning from feedback, cultivating a love for learning, practicing resilience, and fostering gratitude and humility, individuals can shift from a self-centered worldview to one that values personal growth and authentic connections with others. This shift not only benefits the individual but also enriches relationships and contributes to a more empathetic and fulfilling life.

Chapter 14

Mindfulness and Narcissism

How Mindfulness Can Help Curb Narcissistic Behaviors

Mindfulness, the practice of maintaining a moment-by-moment awareness of our thoughts, feelings, bodily sensations, and surrounding environment, can be a powerful tool in addressing and curbing narcissistic behaviors. By promoting self-awareness, emotional regulation, and empathy, mindfulness practices can help individuals recognize and alter patterns of self-centeredness that often characterize narcissism.

Understanding Mindfulness

At its core, mindfulness involves observing one's thoughts and feelings without judgment. This non-reactive awareness allows individuals to step back from their emotions and behaviors, creating space for reflection. For someone struggling with narcissistic tendencies, mindfulness serves as a mirror, reflecting patterns of thought and behavior that may otherwise go unnoticed. It encourages a deeper understanding of how one's actions impact others, fostering a sense of connection rather than isolation.

Enhancing Self-Awareness

One of the primary benefits of mindfulness is increased self-awareness. Narcissistic individuals may often be oblivious to the effects of their actions on others, focusing primarily on their own needs and desires. Mindfulness practices, such as meditation and mindful breathing, can help individuals tune into their internal landscape, recognizing when they are slipping into self-centered thoughts or behaviors.

For example, a daily practice of mindfulness meditation can help in identifying the triggers that provoke narcissistic responses, such as feelings of inadequacy or the need for external validation. By becoming aware of these triggers, individuals can learn to respond differently, choosing to engage in more compassionate and empathetic interactions.

Emotional Regulation

Narcissism is often accompanied by intense emotions, including shame, anger, and a pervasive fear of vulnerability. Mindfulness can aid in managing these emotions by promoting emotional regulation. Through mindfulness techniques, individuals can learn to observe their emotional responses without becoming overwhelmed by them.

For instance, when faced with criticism, a mindful individual can pause and take a breath instead of reacting defensively. This pause allows for reflection and a more measured response, decreasing the likelihood of falling back into narcissistic patterns. Over time, this practice can help in developing a more balanced emotional landscape, where feelings are acknowledged but do not dictate one's actions.

Fostering Empathy

A significant barrier to overcoming narcissistic behavior is the empathy deficit that often accompanies it. Mindfulness can cultivate empathy by encouraging individuals to consider the perspectives and feelings of others. Mindfulness practices often include exercises that promote perspective-taking—such as imagining oneself in another's shoes or reflecting on how one's actions affect others emotionally.

Engaging in loving-kindness meditation, a specific mindfulness technique, can be particularly effective. This practice involves silently repeating phrases that wish well-being and happiness to oneself and others. By regularly practicing loving-kindness, individuals can begin to develop a more authentic sense of compassion, which is essential for combating narcissistic tendencies.

Practical Mindfulness Techniques

To incorporate mindfulness into daily life, individuals can practice:

1. Mindful Breathing: Taking a few minutes each day to focus on breathing can ground individuals in the present moment and help manage overwhelming emotions.

2. Body Scan: This involves paying attention to different parts of the body, which can foster a deeper awareness of physical sensations and emotional states.

3. Journaling: Reflective journaling can help articulate thoughts and feelings, promoting understanding of self-centered patterns and the impact of those behaviors on relationships.

4. Gratitude Practices: Regularly noting things one is grateful for can shift focus from self-centeredness to appreciation for others, which is crucial for developing humility.

By incorporating mindfulness into their lives, individuals struggling with narcissistic behaviors can cultivate a more balanced perspective, improve emotional regulation, and enhance their capacity for empathy, ultimately leading to healthier, more meaningful relationships.

Daily Practices to Cultivate Awareness and Presence

Cultivating awareness and presence in our daily lives is essential for mitigating narcissistic tendencies and fostering healthier relationships with ourselves and others. This process involves intentional practices that help ground us in the present moment, allowing us to observe our thoughts, feelings, and behaviors without judgment. Below are several effective daily practices that can enhance awareness and presence, ultimately contributing to personal growth and emotional well-being.

1. Mindful Breathing

One of the simplest yet most powerful practices for cultivating awareness is mindful breathing. Start your day by dedicating a few minutes to focused breathing. Find a quiet space, sit comfortably, and take deep, intentional breaths. Inhale slowly through your nose, allowing your abdomen to rise, and exhale gently through your mouth. As you breathe, pay attention to the sensations in your body and the rhythm of your breath. If your mind wanders, gently bring it back to the breath. This practice not only calms the mind but also enhances your ability to stay present throughout the day.

2. Journaling

Journaling is an excellent tool for self-reflection and awareness. Set aside time each day to write about your thoughts, feelings, and experiences. Focus on your emotional responses to various situations and how they relate to your beliefs and behaviors. This practice helps you recognize patterns in your thinking that may indicate narcissistic tendencies, such as a need for validation or an unwillingness to acknowledge your imperfections. Journaling encourages honesty with yourself, facilitating a deeper understanding of your motivations and desires.

3. Mindful Observation

Incorporate mindful observation into your daily routine by taking time to notice your surroundings. Whether you are on a walk, in a café, or at home, consciously observe the details of your environment. Engage all your senses—notice the colors, sounds, smells, and textures around you. This practice helps anchor you in the present moment and fosters a sense of appreciation for the world beyond yourself. It can also reduce the tendency to ruminate on personal concerns, shifting your focus outward.

4. Daily Gratitude Practice

Gratitude is a powerful antidote to narcissism, as it encourages a focus on the positive aspects of life and fosters connection with others. Each day, take a moment to list three things you are grateful for, whether they are big or small. Reflect on why you appreciate these aspects and how they contribute to your well-being. Cultivating gratitude shifts your mindset from self-centeredness to appreciation, promoting a healthier perspective on life and relationships.

5. Active Listening
Practicing active listening when engaging with others is crucial for developing empathy and presence. When someone speaks, focus entirely on their words without planning your response or letting your mind wander. Show genuine interest by nodding, maintaining eye contact, and reflecting back what you've heard. This practice not only enhances your connection with others but also helps you become more aware of your own tendencies to dominate conversations or seek validation through your responses.

6. Mindfulness Meditation
Incorporating a formal mindfulness meditation practice into your daily routine can significantly enhance your ability to cultivate awareness. Spend 10-20 minutes each day in meditation, focusing on your breath, body sensations, or a specific mantra. This practice trains your mind to recognize when it drifts into self-referential thinking and encourages a non-judgmental observation of your thoughts.

7. Digital Detox
Finally, consider implementing regular digital detox periods. Social media and constant connectivity can amplify narcissistic tendencies by promoting comparison and the need for validation. Set specific times each day or week to unplug from your devices, allowing yourself to engage more fully with the present moment and the people around you.

In summary, integrating these daily practices into your routine can significantly enhance your awareness and presence, laying the groundwork for personal growth and healthier relationships. By fostering mindfulness, gratitude, and empathy, you can effectively combat narcissistic tendencies and cultivate a more fulfilling, connected life.

Using Meditation to Manage Ego and Narcissistic Tendencies
Meditation is an ancient practice that has gained significant traction in the modern world, particularly as a tool for personal growth and emotional regulation. For individuals struggling with narcissistic tendencies, meditation can serve as a transformative approach to managing the often overwhelming influence of ego. By fostering self-awareness, enhancing emotional regulation, and cultivating compassion, meditation can help individuals move away from self-centered behaviors and toward a more empathetic and balanced existence.

Understanding the Ego
At its core, the ego is a construct of the mind that shapes our identity and self-image. For those

with narcissistic traits, the ego can become inflated, leading to a constant need for validation, admiration, and control. This inflated sense of self often manifests in self-centered behaviors and a lack of empathy for others. To combat these tendencies, it is crucial to develop a healthier relationship with the ego, recognizing its presence without allowing it to dominate one's thoughts and actions.

The Role of Meditation

Meditation offers a pathway to quiet the mind and create space for introspection. Regular practice encourages individuals to observe their thoughts and feelings without judgment. This non-reactive awareness is essential for those with narcissistic tendencies, as it allows them to recognize patterns of self-importance and entitlement. Through meditation, individuals can learn to detach from their ego-driven thoughts and cultivate a more grounded sense of self.

1. Mindfulness Meditation: This practice emphasizes being present in the moment and observing thoughts as they arise. By acknowledging feelings of superiority or the desire for validation without engaging with them, individuals can begin to diminish the power of their ego. Mindfulness fosters a sense of acceptance and compassion toward oneself and others, which is crucial for breaking the cycle of narcissism.

2. Loving-Kindness Meditation (Metta): This form of meditation specifically focuses on developing compassion for oneself and others. By silently repeating phrases of goodwill and kindness, individuals can gradually shift their perspective from self-centeredness to a more inclusive view that recognizes the humanity of others. This practice is particularly beneficial for those with narcissistic tendencies, as it directly combats the emotional disconnect often experienced by narcissists.

3. Body Scan Meditation: This practice encourages individuals to connect with their physical selves, promoting awareness of bodily sensations and emotions. By tuning into the body, practitioners can identify areas of tension associated with ego-driven thoughts and consciously relax these areas. This connection can help anchor individuals, reducing the tendency to become lost in self-importance.

Building Emotional Resilience

Meditation not only aids in managing ego but also enhances emotional resilience. Through consistent practice, individuals can learn to navigate difficult emotions, such as shame or anger, with greater ease. Instead of reacting defensively or seeking external validation, they can respond with curiosity and self-compassion. This emotional intelligence is vital in developing healthier relationships and improving interpersonal dynamics.

Cultivating Gratitude
Incorporating gratitude into meditation can further diminish narcissistic tendencies. By reflecting on the positive aspects of life and acknowledging the contributions of others, individuals can shift their focus away from themselves. Gratitude practices can foster a sense of interconnectedness, encouraging individuals to recognize that their worth is not solely dependent on external validation or achievements.

Conclusion
In conclusion, meditation serves as a powerful tool for managing ego and mitigating narcissistic tendencies. By fostering mindfulness, compassion, and emotional resilience, meditation can help individuals cultivate a more balanced sense of self and improve their relationships with others. As practitioners commit to regular meditation, they can experience a profound transformation, moving toward a more empathetic and fulfilling life. This journey, while challenging, is essential for anyone seeking to break free from the constraints of narcissism and embrace a more authentic existence.

The Role of Gratitude in Shifting Focus Away from Self-Centeredness
Gratitude is a powerful emotional practice that can significantly counteract self-centeredness, a prevalent trait in narcissism. At its core, gratitude involves recognizing and appreciating the positive aspects of life, including the kindness of others, personal achievements, and the beauty of everyday experiences. This simple yet profound shift in focus from the self to the external world can serve as a crucial antidote to narcissistic tendencies, promoting healthier relationships and personal well-being.

Understanding Self-Centeredness
Self-centeredness often manifests as an excessive focus on one's own feelings, needs, and experiences, leading to a distorted perception of reality where one believes they are the center of the universe. Narcissistic individuals may exhibit a constant need for admiration and validation, often disregarding the feelings and needs of others. This myopic view can alienate friends, family, and colleagues, resulting in strained relationships and emotional isolation.

The Transformative Power of Gratitude
Research has shown that practicing gratitude can lead to significant psychological benefits, including increased levels of happiness, improved emotional regulation, and enhanced relationships. By shifting focus from oneself to others, gratitude encourages individuals to acknowledge the support and contributions of those around them. This recognition fosters a sense of connection and belonging, which is often lacking in narcissistic individuals.

1. Cultivating Perspective: Gratitude helps individuals see the bigger picture. When one actively reflects on what they are thankful for, it becomes easier to recognize the efforts and sacrifices made by others. This not only diminishes self-centered thoughts but also promotes empathy—an essential component in building and maintaining relationships.

2. Shifting Attention: Engaging in a gratitude practice can redirect the mind from negative self-talk and self-absorption to positive reflections on life. This shift in attention reduces the pervasive feelings of entitlement that often accompany narcissism. By focusing on what one has rather than what one lacks, the practice of gratitude can foster a more balanced perspective.

3. Enhancing Emotional Awareness: Gratitude encourages emotional awareness by prompting individuals to reflect on their feelings and express appreciation for positive experiences. This process can help those with narcissistic tendencies understand and process their emotions more healthily, moving away from defensiveness and denial.

4. Building Resilience: Regularly practicing gratitude can create a buffer against negative emotions such as envy, resentment, and anger—all of which can fuel narcissistic behaviors. By fostering an attitude of appreciation, individuals become more resilient to life's challenges and are less likely to react with self-centeredness when faced with adversity.

Practical Steps to Cultivate Gratitude

1. Gratitude Journaling: Set aside a few minutes each day to write down three things you are grateful for. This practice encourages reflection and helps solidify positive experiences in memory.

2. Expressing Thanks: Make it a habit to express gratitude to those around you. Whether through verbal acknowledgment, handwritten notes, or small acts of kindness, expressing thanks strengthens social bonds and reinforces an appreciation for others.

3. Mindfulness and Reflection: Incorporate mindfulness practices that focus on gratitude, such as meditation or guided visualizations. These can help deepen the appreciation for life's blessings and enhance emotional regulation.

4. Gratitude Rituals: Create daily or weekly rituals that emphasize gratitude, such as sharing what you appreciate about each other during family meals or community gatherings. This communal practice reinforces connections and fosters a supportive environment.

In conclusion, gratitude serves as a transformative tool for shifting focus away from self-centeredness. By fostering awareness of the contributions and kindness of others, individuals can cultivate empathy, strengthen relationships, and embark on a path toward personal growth and healing from narcissistic traits. The journey to a more fulfilling, interconnected life begins with the simple act of gratitude.

Developing a Practice of Letting Go: Releasing Control and Expectations

In a world that often emphasizes achievement, control, and perfection, the ability to let go can feel counterintuitive. However, for individuals grappling with narcissistic traits, the practice of releasing control and expectations is vital for emotional healing and personal growth. This process not only fosters healthier relationships but also nurtures a more authentic sense of self.

Understanding the Need for Control

At the core of narcissism lies an intense need for control. This desire often stems from underlying insecurities—an attempt to shield oneself from vulnerability and emotional pain. Narcissistic individuals may feel compelled to manage every aspect of their lives and the lives of those around them, fearing that relinquishing control will expose them to criticism or failure. This behavior can manifest in various ways: micromanaging relationships, being overly critical of oneself and others, or insisting on perfection in every endeavor.

Recognizing this pattern is the first step toward letting go. Acknowledging that control is often an illusion can be liberating. The reality is that life is unpredictable, and trying to impose rigid expectations can lead to frustration, disappointment, and a perpetual cycle of self-recrimination.

The Process of Letting Go

Letting go is not a one-time event but a continuous practice that requires patience and self-compassion. **Here are several strategies to help individuals cultivate this essential skill:**

1. Mindfulness and Awareness: Mindfulness encourages individuals to become aware of their thoughts and feelings without judgment. By practicing mindfulness, one can begin to identify moments when they feel the urge to control outcomes or situations. This awareness is crucial for recognizing triggers and fostering a sense of acceptance.

2. Challenging Perfectionism: Perfectionism is often rooted in a fear of inadequacy. Learning to embrace imperfection involves reframing how one views mistakes and failures. Instead of seeing them as reflections of self-worth, consider them opportunities for growth. Engage in self-talk that emphasizes learning and improvement rather than harsh criticism.

3. Setting Realistic Expectations: High expectations can be debilitating. Begin by assessing what is realistically achievable in various aspects of life—work, relationships, and personal goals. Setting smaller, attainable goals can help reduce the pressure to achieve perfection and facilitate a more flexible approach to success.

4. Practicing Gratitude: Gratitude shifts the focus from what is lacking to what is present. Keeping a gratitude journal, where one notes daily moments or aspects of life that bring joy, can help cultivate a mindset of appreciation. This practice encourages individuals to let go of the need for more and to value what they currently have.

5. Embracing Vulnerability: Vulnerability is often viewed as a weakness, but it is, in fact, a source of strength. Allow yourself to be open and honest about your fears and limitations. Sharing these feelings with trusted friends or a therapist can foster deeper connections and create space for healing.

6. Engaging in Compassionate Self-Talk: Replace negative self-talk with messages of kindness and understanding. Acknowledge your struggles without judgment. Remind yourself that it is okay to be human, and that everyone has their own battles. This shift can alleviate the pressure to control every situation and allow for a more nurturing internal dialogue.

7. Letting Go of the Need for Validation: Many individuals with narcissistic traits seek external validation to confirm their self-worth. Learning to derive self-esteem from within, rather than from external sources, is crucial for releasing control. Engage in activities that promote intrinsic satisfaction, such as pursuing hobbies or volunteering, which can provide a sense of fulfillment independent of others' opinions.

Conclusion

Developing a practice of letting go is an essential component of healing from narcissistic traits. By releasing control and expectations, individuals can cultivate deeper connections, foster self-compassion, and ultimately lead a more authentic and fulfilling life. This journey requires ongoing commitment, but through mindfulness, gratitude, and vulnerability, it becomes possible to embrace the beauty of imperfection and the freedom of acceptance.

Chapter 15

Narcissism in the Age of Social Media

How Social Media Reinforces Narcissism

In the contemporary digital landscape, social media platforms have become ubiquitous, shaping how individuals communicate, express themselves, and perceive their own identities. While these platforms can foster connections and community, they also have a propensity to reinforce narcissistic behaviors and traits among users. Understanding this phenomenon requires a closer examination of the mechanisms through which social media cultivates self-centeredness, the pursuit of validation, and the impact on interpersonal relationships.

One of the most significant ways social media reinforces narcissism is through the immediate feedback loop it creates. Users post images, statuses, and videos with the hope of receiving likes, shares, and comments. This quest for validation can become addictive, as each notification serves as a dopamine hit, encouraging individuals to seek more attention and approval. The constant reinforcement of positive feedback can exacerbate narcissistic tendencies, leading individuals to prioritize their online personas over authentic self-representation. As a result, many users curate their lives meticulously, focusing on showcasing only their most glamorous moments while downplaying vulnerabilities or failures.

Moreover, social media promotes a culture of comparison, where individuals are constantly measuring their worth against the carefully crafted lives of others. This comparison often leads to feelings of inadequacy and the need to portray an inflated self-image. People may engage in self-promotion, highlighting achievements, possessions, and lifestyles that project an idealized version of themselves. This behavior is particularly prevalent among individuals with narcissistic traits, as they often seek external validation to bolster their self-esteem. The need to appear superior or more successful than peers can ultimately create a toxic environment, fostering competition instead of genuine connections.

The algorithms that govern social media platforms further exacerbate these tendencies by prioritizing content that generates high engagement—often sensational or self-aggrandizing posts. This dynamic creates echo chambers where narcissistic behaviors are not only encouraged but rewarded. Users may feel pressured to conform to these standards, leading to a cycle of self-centered content creation that emphasizes superficiality over substance. As individuals vie for attention, they may neglect meaningful interactions, fostering a sense of isolation despite being more "connected" than ever.

Additionally, the transient nature of social media interactions can diminish the value of relationships. The emphasis on likes and shares often overshadows genuine emotional connection, leading to shallow interactions that lack depth. When relationships are reduced to metrics of popularity, individuals may struggle to develop empathy and meaningful bonds, further entrenching narcissistic behaviors. This lack of emotional engagement can lead to difficulties in real-life relationships, as individuals may find themselves ill-equipped to navigate the complexities of face-to-face interactions.

Finally, the phenomenon of "cancel culture" and public shaming on social media can ironically reinforce narcissism by driving individuals to defend their self-image at all costs. When criticized, those with narcissistic tendencies may react defensively or retaliate, using social media to either attack their critics or amplify their victimhood. This cycle of blame and self-justification is detrimental not only to personal growth but also to the overall health of online communities.

In conclusion, while social media has the potential to connect individuals and foster community, it simultaneously reinforces narcissistic behaviors through validation-seeking, superficial relationships, and the culture of comparison. To mitigate these influences, it is essential for individuals to cultivate self-awareness and mindfulness about their social media usage, striving for authentic engagement rather than mere validation. By doing so, users can work towards healthier interactions both online and in their everyday lives, ultimately breaking the cycle of narcissism that social media can perpetuate.

The Constant Need for Validation Online

In today's digital age, social media platforms serve as the primary stage for self-expression, interaction, and validation. The constant need for validation online has become a prevalent issue, particularly among individuals with narcissistic traits, but it can affect anyone who engages with these platforms. Understanding the mechanics behind this need is essential in recognizing its impact on mental health and interpersonal relationships.

The Mechanisms of Online Validation

Social media platforms like Instagram, Facebook, Twitter, and TikTok are designed to foster engagement. Users post photos, status updates, and videos, often seeking feedback in the form of likes, comments, and shares. This feedback can trigger the release of dopamine, a neurotransmitter associated with pleasure and reward. Each notification serves as a small validation boost, affirming one's self-worth and reinforcing the behavior of seeking more attention.

For individuals with narcissistic traits, this need for external validation can be amplified. The validation received from online interactions can feel more immediate and gratifying than traditional forms of affirmation. Likes and comments become a measure of one's desirability and popularity, which can lead to a cycle of compulsive posting and checking for reactions. This cycle not only reinforces narcissistic behaviors but can also lead to emotional instability when the anticipated validation does not materialize.

Impacts on Self-Perception and Mental Health

The reliance on online validation can distort self-perception. Individuals may find themselves equating their self-worth with the number of likes or positive comments they receive. This can create a fragile sense of self, where feelings of inadequacy surface if a post does not perform well. Over time, this can lead to increased anxiety, depression, and a pervasive fear of rejection. The pressure to maintain a curated online persona can become overwhelming, often leading to burnout.

In addition, the comparison culture fostered by social media exacerbates feelings of inadequacy. Users frequently compare themselves to others based on curated images and highlights. This comparison can be detrimental, leading to feelings of jealousy and resentment, further feeding into the need for validation. The cycle of seeking approval and experiencing discontent can create a toxic emotional environment, hindering personal growth and fostering deeper insecurities.

Balancing Online Presence with Authenticity

To mitigate the negative effects of seeking validation online, individuals must strive for a more balanced approach. Here are several strategies:

1. Mindful Engagement: Be aware of your motivations for posting. Ask yourself whether you're sharing to express yourself authentically or simply to gain likes and comments. Mindfulness can help cultivate a healthier relationship with social media.

2. Limit Social Media Use: Set boundaries around your social media usage. Designate specific times for checking accounts and reduce the frequency of posts. This can help lessen the compulsive need for validation.

3. Cultivate Internal Validation: Shift focus from external validation to internal validation. Engage in self-reflection and recognize your inherent worth beyond social media metrics. Practice self-compassion and affirmations to develop a positive self-image that is not contingent on online feedback.

4. Seek Real-Life Connections: Foster relationships in real life rather than relying solely on online interactions. Engaging in face-to-face conversations can provide a deeper sense of connection and fulfillment that online validation cannot replicate.

5. Unplug Regularly: Take breaks from social media to reassess your relationship with it. Unplugging can provide clarity and help you reconnect with what truly matters in your life, reducing the dependency on online validation.

Conclusion

The constant need for validation online is a reflection of broader societal trends and can significantly impact self-esteem and mental health. By understanding the dynamics of this need and implementing strategies to cultivate a healthier relationship with social media, individuals can break free from the cycle of seeking external approval, fostering a more authentic and fulfilling life.

Balancing Self-Promotion with Authenticity

In an increasingly competitive world, self-promotion has become an essential skill for personal and professional development. However, the line between effective self-promotion and narcissism can often blur, leading individuals to prioritize image over authenticity. Striking a balance between showcasing one's achievements and remaining true to oneself is crucial for fostering genuine connections and ensuring long-term success.

Understanding Self-Promotion

Self-promotion involves highlighting one's skills, achievements, and experiences to gain recognition, credibility, or opportunities. In today's society, particularly with the rise of social media and professional networking platforms, the ability to market oneself has never been more critical. However, this necessity can lead to excessive self-focus, where individuals may feel pressured to curate an idealized version of themselves.

Authenticity, on the other hand, encompasses being genuine, transparent, and true to one's values and beliefs. When one is authentic, the message conveyed resonates more deeply with others, fostering trust and respect. Authentic self-promotion does not merely showcase achievements but also reflects the individual's unique journey, values, and beliefs.

The Risks of Excessive Self-Promotion

Engaging in excessive self-promotion can lead to perceptions of narcissism, which may alienate others. Narcissistic tendencies often manifest as a constant need for admiration and validation, overshadowing the importance of humility and empathy. When individuals focus too heavily on their accomplishments without considering the perspectives of others, they risk appearing self-centered.

Moreover, the pressure to maintain an image can create a façade that is unsustainable. Individuals may feel compelled to exaggerate their achievements or downplay their vulnerabilities, leading to a loss of authenticity. This disconnection can result in feelings of isolation, anxiety, and dissatisfaction, as the individual feels they must continuously uphold a false persona.

Strategies for Balancing Self-Promotion and Authenticity

1. Embrace Vulnerability: Sharing not only successes but also challenges and failures can enhance authenticity. Discussing setbacks allows others to relate to your journey, fostering a sense of connection and mutual understanding. Vulnerability can humanize your narrative and encourage others to share their experiences, creating a supportive community.

2. Focus on Value Creation: Rather than merely promoting oneself, consider how your skills and experiences can benefit others. Shift the focus from "Look what I've done" to "How can I help you?" This approach cultivates a sense of service and contribution, reinforcing the idea that self-promotion can coexist with a genuine desire to support others.

3. Practice Self-Reflection: Regularly assess your motivations behind self-promotion. Are you seeking validation or recognition, or are you genuinely excited to share your journey? Engaging in self-reflection can help ensure that your self-promotion aligns with your values and purpose, keeping authenticity at the forefront.

4. Seek Feedback: Open yourself to constructive criticism from trusted friends or colleagues. They can provide insights into how your self-promotion is perceived and help you identify areas where you could enhance your authenticity. This feedback loop can guide you in refining your approach and ensuring that your self-promotion resonates with others.

5. Cultivate Empathy: Develop the ability to see things from others' perspectives when promoting yourself. Consider how your achievements may impact your audience and frame your narrative in a way that acknowledges their experiences. This empathetic approach can create a more inclusive atmosphere, allowing you to connect on a deeper level.

Conclusion
Balancing self-promotion with authenticity is an ongoing journey that requires mindfulness

and self-awareness. By embracing vulnerability, focusing on value creation, engaging in self-reflection, seeking feedback, and cultivating empathy, individuals can successfully navigate the complexities of self-promotion. Ultimately, fostering genuine connections grounded in authenticity not only enriches personal and professional relationships but also leads to a more fulfilling and meaningful life.

Developing a Healthy Relationship with Social Media

In today's digital age, social media has become an integral part of our lives, shaping how we communicate, share, and perceive ourselves and others. While it offers numerous benefits, such as connectivity and information sharing, it can also contribute to narcissistic tendencies and self-centered behavior. Developing a healthy relationship with social media is crucial for maintaining emotional well-being and fostering authentic connections.

Understanding the Impact of Social Media

Social media platforms are designed to promote engagement and interaction, often leading to a culture of comparison and validation. Users frequently measure their self-worth by the number of likes, comments, and followers they receive. This external validation can create a cycle of dependency, where individuals feel compelled to curate their online personas to gain approval, thereby reinforcing narcissistic traits.

Moreover, the constant exposure to idealized portrayals of others' lives can lead to feelings of inadequacy and envy. When individuals compare their behind-the-scenes struggles to the highlight reels of others, it can exacerbate feelings of shame and guilt. Recognizing these dynamics is the first step toward cultivating a healthier relationship with social media.

Setting Boundaries

To cultivate a healthy relationship with social media, it's essential to set boundaries around its use. This can include limiting the amount of time spent on social media platforms, creating specific times of day for checking updates, or even designating social media-free zones in your home. By establishing these boundaries, you create space for more meaningful, face-to-face interactions and activities that promote personal growth.

Additionally, curating your social media feeds to include accounts that inspire and uplift rather than invoke jealousy or negativity can significantly impact your emotional landscape. Follow individuals and organizations that promote authenticity, mental health, and compassion, and unfollow those that contribute to feelings of inadequacy or comparison.

Fostering Authenticity
Authenticity is key to developing a healthy relationship with social media. Rather than presenting a curated version of yourself that seeks validation, embrace vulnerability and share your true experiences. This can help you connect with others on a deeper level, fostering relationships based on empathy and understanding rather than surface-level interaction.

Engaging in honest conversations about mental health, challenges, and personal growth can encourage others to do the same. By promoting a culture of authenticity, you contribute to a more supportive online environment that prioritizes interpersonal connection over superficial engagement.

Balancing Self-Promotion with Humility
While social media can be a platform for self-promotion, it's essential to strike a balance between showcasing achievements and maintaining humility. Recognize that it's perfectly acceptable to share successes, but do so in a way that invites dialogue and connection rather than competition. Celebrate the accomplishments of others and offer support, which can help shift the focus from self-centeredness to community building.

Practicing gratitude is also vital. Regularly reflecting on what you appreciate in your life, including the people and experiences that bring you joy, can help shift your focus away from self-promotion. Gratitude can cultivate a sense of fulfillment that doesn't rely on external validation.

Unplugging for Mental Health
Finally, it's crucial to recognize when social media usage may be negatively impacting your mental health. Taking regular breaks or unplugging entirely can help you reconnect with yourself and the world around you. Engage in offline activities that bring you joy, such as reading, exercising, or spending time with loved ones. This not only helps to ground you but also allows you to cultivate deeper relationships without the distractions that social media can present.

In conclusion, developing a healthy relationship with social media requires mindfulness, intentionality, and a commitment to authenticity. By setting boundaries, fostering genuine connections, and practicing gratitude, you can navigate the complexities of social media without falling prey to its potential pitfalls, ultimately leading to a more balanced and fulfilling life.

Unplugging: How to Disconnect for Mental Health
In an age where digital connectivity is ubiquitous, the phenomenon of social media has

transformed the way we interact, perceive ourselves, and relate to others. While these platforms can foster relationships and provide a space for self-expression, they often exacerbate feelings of self-centeredness and narcissism. The constant barrage of curated images, likes, and comments creates an environment ripe for comparison and validation-seeking behavior. As such, learning to unplug from these digital distractions is not merely beneficial; it is essential for maintaining mental health and cultivating a more balanced, empathetic lifestyle.

The Impact of Digital Overload

Our brains are not wired to handle the overwhelming volume of information and social interactions that modern technology presents. Continuous exposure to social media can lead to increased anxiety, depression, and feelings of inadequacy. The pressure to present a perfect image online can lead to distorted self-perceptions and a diminished sense of self-worth. This digital overload also detracts from our ability to engage in meaningful face-to-face interactions, which are crucial for building genuine relationships and fostering emotional intimacy.

Steps to Unplug

1. Establish Boundaries: One of the first steps to disconnecting is to set clear boundaries around technology use. Determine specific times of the day when you will engage with social media or check emails. For instance, you might choose to limit screen time to one hour in the evening, ensuring that the rest of your time can be devoted to more enriching activities.

2. Digital Detox: Consider implementing a digital detox, which involves taking a break from all electronic devices for a designated period. This could be as short as a weekend or as long as a month. During this time, focus on non-digital pursuits such as reading, hiking, or spending quality time with loved ones. Document your experience in a journal to reflect on how it impacts your mental well-being.

3. Mindful Consumption: When you do engage with technology, practice mindful consumption. Be intentional about the content you consume and the accounts you follow. Choose to engage with uplifting, educational, and positive material instead of content that fuels negativity or comparison. This conscious choice can mitigate the adverse effects of social media exposure.

4. Cultivating Offline Connections: Make a concerted effort to strengthen your offline relationships. Schedule regular meetups with friends or family without the distraction of phones. Engage in activities that promote connection, such as cooking together, playing board games, or participating in community events. These interactions will help cultivate empathy and genuine relationships, counteracting the isolating effects of online engagement.

5. Engaging in Nature: Nature has a profound effect on mental health and well-being. Spend time outdoors, whether it's a walk in the park, a hike in the woods, or simply sitting in your backyard. Nature not only provides a serene backdrop for reflection but also helps ground you in the present moment, reducing the influence of digital distractions.

6. Practicing Mindfulness and Meditation: Incorporating mindfulness and meditation into your daily routine can significantly enhance your ability to disconnect from digital stimuli. Techniques such as focused breathing, body scans, or guided meditations can cultivate a greater awareness of your thoughts and feelings, helping you to detach from the constant pull of online engagement.

Benefits of Unplugging

Disconnecting from technology allows you to reconnect with yourself and the world around you. It encourages self-reflection, promotes emotional stability, and nurtures your capacity for empathy. By reducing the noise of social media, you create space for authentic experiences and relationships, ultimately leading to a more fulfilling and balanced life. Additionally, unplugging fosters a healthier relationship with technology, allowing you to engage with it in a way that supports your mental health rather than detracts from it.

In conclusion, the act of unplugging is a vital tool in combating narcissistic tendencies and fostering mental well-being. By implementing practical strategies to disconnect, you can reclaim your time, enhance your self-awareness, and cultivate deeper connections with those around you.

Chapter 16

Emotional Healing and Growth

The Emotional Toll of Narcissism: Shame, Guilt, and Anger

Narcissism, characterized by an inflated sense of self-importance and a deep need for admiration, often masks profound emotional vulnerabilities. While individuals exhibiting narcissistic traits may project confidence and superiority, beneath this façade lies a complex emotional landscape filled with shame, guilt, and anger. Understanding these emotions is crucial for both individuals struggling with narcissistic tendencies and those affected by narcissism in their relationships.

Shame is a pervasive emotional experience for many who struggle with narcissism. It often stems from an internal recognition that one's self-image is not as grand as they would like to portray. This dissonance can lead to a chronic sense of inadequacy, which narcissists may attempt to cover up through various means, including arrogance, entitlement, or even aggression. For many, the fear of being exposed as flawed or unworthy can result in defensive behaviors aimed at maintaining a protected self-image. This cycle can perpetuate feelings of shame, as the narcissist feels compelled to continue acting out these traits to avoid confronting their vulnerabilities.

In contrast, guilt arises when one's actions negatively impact others. Narcissists may engage in behaviors that are self-serving, often at the expense of their relationships. When confronted with the consequences of their actions, they may feel guilt. However, this guilt is often fleeting and quickly transformed into blame or defensiveness. This inability to sustain genuine guilt can hinder personal growth and repair damaged relationships, as the focus shifts away from accountability toward self-preservation. The transition from guilt to defensiveness can create a toxic cycle, where the narcissist fails to learn from their mistakes, perpetuating harm to themselves and others.

Anger is another prevalent emotion associated with narcissism. This anger can manifest in various forms, including frustration, rage, or passive-aggressive behavior. Often, it stems from perceived slights or criticisms, provoking a defensive response. Narcissists may react violently to situations that challenge their self-esteem, leading to conflicts in personal and professional relationships. This anger, however, is often a mask for deeper emotional wounds, including feelings of inadequacy and rejection. When faced with vulnerability, instead of processing these emotions constructively, they may lash out, further alienating themselves from others.

The interplay of shame, guilt, and anger creates a complex emotional burden for individuals grappling with narcissistic traits. This emotional toll is not only detrimental to the individual but also significantly impacts their relationships. Partners, family members, and friends often find themselves navigating the turbulent waters of a narcissistic individual's emotional landscape, which can lead to their own feelings of confusion, hurt, and resentment. The inability of the narcissist to acknowledge and process shame, guilt, and anger can result in a cycle of emotional abuse, leaving others feeling invalidated and unworthy.

For healing to occur, it is essential for individuals with narcissistic tendencies to confront these difficult emotions. Acknowledging feelings of shame, guilt, and anger as legitimate experiences is the first step toward emotional growth. Therapy can be a powerful tool in this journey, providing a safe space to explore these emotions without judgment. Through therapeutic intervention, individuals can learn to navigate their emotional landscape, develop healthier coping mechanisms, and cultivate genuine empathy toward themselves and others.

In summary, the emotional toll of narcissism is significant, affecting not only the individuals who exhibit these traits but also those around them. By understanding and addressing the underlying shame, guilt, and anger, individuals can begin the process of healing, ultimately leading to healthier relationships and a more authentic sense of self.

Learning to Process Difficult Emotions

Processing difficult emotions is a crucial step in healing narcissistic tendencies and fostering emotional growth. Emotions such as shame, guilt, anger, and sadness can be overwhelming and often lead to maladaptive responses, including defensiveness, withdrawal, or even aggression. For individuals struggling with narcissism, these emotions can trigger a cycle of self-centered behavior as they attempt to shield themselves from feelings of inadequacy or vulnerability. However, learning to effectively process these emotions can pave the way for greater self-awareness, healthier relationships, and a more fulfilling life.

Understanding Difficult Emotions

Difficult emotions are an inherent part of the human experience. They serve as indicators of our internal state and can provide valuable insights into our needs, desires, and boundaries. Shame may arise from feelings of failure or unworthiness, while guilt often stems from a sense of responsibility for harming others or failing to meet expectations. Anger, on the other hand, can signal a violation of personal boundaries or an unmet need. Recognizing that these emotions are natural responses to our experiences is the first step in learning to process them effectively.

Acknowledging and Validating Emotions

The process of emotional processing begins with acknowledgment. It is essential to recognize when difficult emotions arise and to validate them by understanding that it is okay to feel this way. This acknowledgment can be facilitated through mindfulness practices, where individuals learn to observe their thoughts and feelings without judgment. Mindfulness encourages a non-reactive stance, allowing space for emotions to be felt and understood rather than suppressed or ignored.

Techniques for Processing Difficult Emotions

1. Journaling: Writing about your feelings can provide a safe outlet for expression. Journaling helps clarify thoughts and emotions, allowing for reflection and insight. It can also reveal patterns in emotional responses, providing a basis for understanding triggers and developing coping strategies.

2. Emotional Regulation Strategies: Techniques such as deep breathing, progressive muscle relaxation, or grounding exercises can help manage overwhelming emotions. These strategies promote physiological calmness, making it easier to face challenging feelings.

3. Talking It Out: Engaging in conversations with trusted friends, family members, or therapists can be incredibly beneficial. Verbalizing emotions can provide relief and foster a sense of connection. It also invites external perspectives that can challenge distorted thinking patterns typical in narcissism.

4. Creative Expression: Art, music, or other creative outlets can serve as powerful tools for processing emotions. Engaging in creative activities provides a means to express feelings in a non-verbal way, which can be particularly beneficial for those who struggle to articulate their emotions.

5. Mindfulness and Meditation: Practicing mindfulness meditation helps cultivate awareness of the present moment, allowing individuals to observe their emotions without becoming overwhelmed. This practice encourages acceptance and can reduce the intensity of difficult emotions.

The Importance of Self-Compassion

As individuals navigate their emotional landscape, self-compassion is key. It involves treating oneself with the same kindness and understanding that one would offer to a friend. Self-compassion mitigates the harsh self-criticism often associated with narcissistic tendencies and allows for a gentler approach to accepting one's imperfections and failures.

Moving Forward

Processing difficult emotions is not a linear journey; it requires patience, practice, and commitment. As individuals learn to navigate their emotional responses, they will likely find that their relationships with themselves and others improve. This newfound emotional resilience fosters deeper connections, cultivates empathy, and encourages a more authentic, fulfilling life. Ultimately, embracing and processing difficult emotions can lead to profound personal growth, breaking the cycle of narcissism and allowing for a richer emotional experience.

Releasing Negative Patterns and Creating New Emotional Habits

The journey towards healing from narcissistic traits involves a critical process of recognizing and releasing negative emotional patterns that have been entrenched over time. These patterns often stem from childhood experiences, learned behaviors, and coping mechanisms developed in response to emotional wounds. To move towards a healthier self-concept and improve interpersonal relationships, it is essential to identify these patterns and actively work to transform them.

Understanding Negative Patterns

Negative emotional patterns often manifest as repetitive cycles of behavior that can hinder personal growth and emotional well-being. These might include tendencies towards defensiveness, a constant need for validation, perfectionism, or an exaggerated sense of entitlement. They can lead to feelings of shame, guilt, and frustration, further entrenching the individual in a cycle of negative self-worth and isolation.

To begin the process of releasing these negative patterns, self-awareness is crucial. This can be achieved through various techniques such as journaling, meditation, or engaging in therapeutic conversations. By reflecting on situations where these patterns emerge, individuals can start to recognize triggers and the emotional responses that follow. This heightened awareness forms the first step towards change.

Creating New Emotional Habits

Once negative patterns are identified, the next step is to replace them with healthier emotional habits. Here are several strategies to facilitate this transformation:

1. Mindfulness Practice: Incorporating mindfulness into daily routines helps cultivate a non-judgmental awareness of thoughts and feelings. This practice allows individuals to observe their emotional responses without reacting impulsively. By learning to pause and reflect, one can choose healthier responses rather than defaulting to negative patterns.

2. Cognitive Restructuring: This involves challenging and changing unhelpful thought patterns. For example, if an individual frequently feels inadequate or unworthy, they can actively replace these thoughts with affirmations of self-worth and capabilities. This cognitive shift not only changes how one perceives themselves but also influences emotional responses.

3. Emotional Regulation Techniques: Developing skills to manage and regulate emotions is critical. Techniques such as deep breathing, progressive muscle relaxation, or grounding exercises can help manage anxiety or anger that may arise from triggering situations. These skills allow for more measured responses rather than reactive behaviors.

4. Setting Intentional Goals: Establishing clear, achievable goals related to emotional health can provide direction in the healing process. This may involve setting intentions for daily practices of gratitude, empathy, or vulnerability. Tracking progress towards these goals fosters a sense of accomplishment and reinforces positive changes.

5. Building a Support System: Surrounding oneself with supportive individuals who encourage healthy emotional expression and accountability can make a significant difference. Sharing experiences and learning from others can provide new perspectives and reinforce the commitment to change.

6. Practice Self-Compassion: It is vital to recognize that change takes time and effort. Practicing self-compassion helps individuals forgive themselves for past mistakes and encourages a more positive self-dialogue. Understanding that everyone is flawed and that growth is an ongoing journey can alleviate the pressure of perfectionism.

In conclusion, releasing negative emotional patterns and creating new habits is a transformative process requiring dedication and self-reflection. By employing mindfulness, cognitive restructuring, emotional regulation, intentional goal-setting, and fostering supportive relationships, individuals can break free from the confines of narcissistic behavior. This journey not only leads to personal healing but also paves the way for more authentic, empathetic connections with others, fostering a more fulfilling life devoid of narcissism.

How Self-Compassion Leads to Emotional Growth

Self-compassion is a powerful tool for fostering emotional growth, particularly for individuals grappling with narcissistic tendencies. At its core, self-compassion involves treating oneself with the same kindness, concern, and support one would offer a good friend. Research in psychology has shown that self-compassionate individuals experience greater emotional resilience, reduced anxiety, and improved overall well-being. This framework is especially crucial for those who may be caught in a cycle of self-criticism and perfectionism, common traits among narcissistic individuals.

Understanding Self-Compassion

Self-compassion is composed of three primary components: self-kindness, common humanity, and mindfulness. Self-kindness encourages individuals to be gentle and understanding toward themselves rather than harshly critical. Common humanity recognizes that suffering and personal inadequacy are part of the shared human experience, allowing individuals to feel connected rather than isolated in their struggles. Mindfulness involves maintaining a balanced awareness of one's emotions, acknowledging painful feelings without over-identifying with them.

Breaking the Cycle of Self-Criticism

For individuals with narcissistic traits, self-criticism can be a significant barrier to emotional growth. This self-criticism often stems from a fear of inadequacy or failure, which can perpetuate a cycle of shame and insecurity. When individuals practice self-compassion, they learn to replace negative self-talk with a supportive inner dialogue. This shift allows them to confront their flaws and failures without judgment, fostering an environment conducive to emotional healing.

By acknowledging that everyone has imperfections and that it's okay to be flawed, individuals can begin to let go of the need for perfectionism that often accompanies narcissistic behavior. This acceptance is crucial for emotional growth, as it opens the door to vulnerability and the exploration of deeper emotional experiences.

Developing Emotional Resilience

Self-compassion directly contributes to emotional resilience—the ability to bounce back from setbacks and cope with challenges effectively. When individuals treat themselves with compassion during difficult times, they are less likely to become overwhelmed by negative emotions such as shame, anger, and guilt. Instead, they can respond to adversity with a sense of understanding and patience, which fosters a healthier relationship with their emotions.

This resilience is particularly vital for those dealing with narcissistic injuries—emotional wounds that can provoke defensive or self-centered responses. By cultivating self-compassion, individuals can learn to approach these injuries with a healing mindset, allowing them to process their feelings constructively rather than reactively.

Building a Foundation for Growth

The journey of emotional growth facilitated by self-compassion also involves learning to forgive oneself for past mistakes. Narcissistic individuals often struggle with self-forgiveness, leading to a cycle of shame and self-punishment. Self-compassion encourages individuals to acknowledge their mistakes without allowing those mistakes to define their self-worth. This process helps in building a more accurate self-image—one that is grounded in authenticity rather than an inflated sense of self.

As individuals learn to accept their imperfections and forgive themselves, they become more open to growth and change. This openness is vital for developing healthier relationships with others, as self-compassion fosters empathy and understanding.

Conclusion
In summary, self-compassion plays a pivotal role in emotional growth, especially for those struggling with narcissistic tendencies. By embracing self-kindness, recognizing shared humanity, and practicing mindfulness, individuals can break free from the destructive cycles of self-criticism and perfectionism. This journey not only enhances emotional resilience but also paves the way for deeper connections with oneself and others. Ultimately, cultivating self-compassion is a transformative practice that fosters healing, emotional stability, and genuine personal growth.

Finding Inner Peace: Long-Term Emotional Health Strategies
Achieving inner peace is a fundamental aspect of emotional health, especially for individuals grappling with narcissistic tendencies. The journey towards inner peace involves a multifaceted approach that prioritizes self-awareness, emotional regulation, and the development of healthy relationships. Here, we outline several long-term strategies that can help cultivate a sense of tranquility and emotional stability.

1. Mindfulness Practices
Mindfulness is a powerful tool for promoting inner peace. By focusing on the present moment and observing thoughts and feelings without judgment, individuals can reduce anxiety and stress. Practices such as meditation, deep breathing exercises, and yoga encourage a state of awareness that helps to calm the mind. Regular engagement in mindfulness can lead to improved emotional regulation, allowing individuals to respond to triggers with greater composure rather than reactivity.

2. Emotional Regulation Techniques
Understanding and managing emotions is crucial for long-term emotional health. Techniques such as identifying emotional triggers, labeling feelings, and practicing self-soothing can help individuals navigate intense emotional experiences. Journaling can serve as a constructive outlet, enabling individuals to articulate their feelings and reflect on their responses. Over time, developing the ability to regulate emotions can lead to greater emotional resilience and a more peaceful state of mind.

3. Building Healthy Relationships
Nurturing supportive and empathetic relationships is essential for emotional well-being. Engaging in open communication, practicing active listening, and fostering mutual respect within relationships can enhance connection and trust. Setting boundaries is also critical; it protects emotional health and allows individuals to engage in relationships that are nourishing rather than depleting. Healthy relationships contribute to a sense of belonging and understanding, essential components of inner peace.

4. Practicing Gratitude

Gratitude shifts focus from what is lacking to what is present and valued in life. Developing a daily gratitude practice—whether through journaling or simply reflecting on positive aspects of life—can foster a more optimistic outlook. This practice helps individuals recognize the abundance in their lives, which can counteract feelings of inadequacy or jealousy often associated with narcissistic tendencies.

5. Self-Compassion and Forgiveness

Cultivating self-compassion allows individuals to treat themselves with the same kindness they would offer a friend. It involves recognizing one's imperfections and mistakes without harsh self-criticism. This practice can be particularly healing for those who have experienced narcissistic injuries. Additionally, learning to forgive oneself is crucial in letting go of past mistakes, which can lighten emotional burdens and promote a sense of inner peace.

6. Creating a Personal Growth Plan

Establishing a clear personal growth plan can provide direction and purpose. Setting realistic, attainable goals encourages individuals to focus on positive change and personal development, reducing the fixation on external validation. Regularly reviewing and adjusting these goals helps maintain motivation and accountability, fostering a sense of accomplishment that contributes to emotional well-being.

7. Engaging in Community Service

Volunteering or engaging in community service can provide a profound sense of fulfillment and connection to others. Serving those in need shifts the focus away from self-centeredness and cultivates empathy and compassion. This sense of contribution can lead to deeper feelings of purpose and satisfaction, enhancing overall emotional health.

8. Therapeutic Support

Seeking professional help through therapy can provide invaluable support in the journey toward inner peace. Therapeutic approaches such as Cognitive Behavioral Therapy (CBT) can help individuals identify and alter negative thought patterns, while group therapy fosters a sense of connection and shared experience. A therapist can guide individuals in developing effective coping strategies tailored to their unique emotional needs.

In summary, finding inner peace is an ongoing process that requires commitment and practice. By integrating mindfulness, emotional regulation, healthy relationships, gratitude, self-compassion, personal growth, community service, and therapeutic support into daily life, individuals can cultivate a lasting sense of tranquility and emotional health. These strategies not only enhance personal well-being but also contribute to more authentic and fulfilling interactions with others.

Chapter 17

Rebuilding Your Life After Narcissism

The Importance of Accountability in Personal Growth

Accountability is a cornerstone of personal growth, particularly for individuals grappling with narcissistic tendencies. It involves taking responsibility for one's actions, thoughts, and emotions and recognizing how these elements impact oneself and others. In the context of overcoming narcissism, accountability serves as a vital tool for fostering self-awareness and facilitating meaningful change.

Understanding Accountability

At its core, accountability means owning up to one's behaviors and the consequences that arise from them. It requires a commitment to honesty, both with oneself and with others. For individuals with narcissistic traits, this can be particularly challenging. Narcissism often thrives on denial, defensiveness, and external blame, leading to a distorted self-image that can hinder personal development. By embracing accountability, individuals can begin to dismantle these barriers and confront their behaviors authentically.

Fostering Self-Awareness

Self-awareness is the bedrock of personal growth. It involves recognizing one's feelings, motives, and triggers. When individuals hold themselves accountable, they engage in a process of reflection that unveils the patterns of their behavior. This reflection can be facilitated through journaling, therapy, or discussions with trusted friends or mentors. Through these practices, individuals can begin to understand how their narcissistic traits manifest in their relationships, leading to greater insight into their emotional landscape.

Encouraging Responsibility

Accountability goes hand-in-hand with responsibility. By acknowledging their part in relationship dynamics and conflicts, individuals can shift from a victim mindset to one of empowerment. This shift is crucial for personal growth, as it empowers individuals to make conscious choices that align with their values and aspirations. When individuals accept responsibility for their actions, they gain control over their narrative and can actively participate in their transformation.

Building Trust in Relationships

Accountability is essential for rebuilding and maintaining trust in relationships. When individuals take responsibility for their actions, they demonstrate respect and consideration for others. This is particularly important for those with narcissistic tendencies, as their behaviors can often lead to emotional harm in relationships. By openly acknowledging their mistakes and working to rectify them, individuals can foster an environment of openness and healing. This not only strengthens their relationships but also reinforces their commitment to personal growth.

Setting Realistic Goals

In the journey of personal growth, setting achievable goals is vital. However, without accountability, it can be easy to lose sight of those objectives. Accountability partners, whether they are friends, family members, or therapists, can provide the support and encouragement needed to stay on track. By regularly checking in on progress, individuals can maintain focus and motivation, ensuring that they are actively working towards their goals rather than slipping back into old habits.

Cultivating a Growth Mindset

Finally, accountability nurtures a growth mindset. It encourages individuals to view mistakes as opportunities for learning rather than as failures. This perspective fosters resilience and a willingness to engage in self-improvement. For those who may struggle with perfectionism—a common trait among narcissists—embracing accountability can help temper unrealistic expectations and promote a healthier approach to personal development.

Conclusion

In summary, accountability is a critical component of personal growth for those struggling with narcissism. By embracing responsibility, fostering self-awareness, building trust in relationships, setting realistic goals, and cultivating a growth mindset, individuals can pave the way for meaningful change. Ultimately, accountability empowers individuals to break free from the constraints of narcissistic behavior, leading to a more authentic, fulfilling life marked by empathy and genuine connection with others.

Taking Responsibility for Past Mistakes

Taking responsibility for past mistakes is a crucial step in personal growth, particularly for individuals struggling with narcissistic traits. This process not only fosters self-awareness but also encourages accountability, ultimately leading to healthier relationships and a more fulfilling life. Acknowledging our missteps can be challenging, especially for those who may have developed a defensive posture towards criticism and vulnerability. However, embracing this responsibility is essential for healing and transformation.

Understanding the Importance of Accountability

Accountability involves recognizing that our actions have consequences, both for ourselves and for others. For individuals with narcissistic tendencies, this acknowledgment can be particularly difficult. Narcissism often thrives on a denial of responsibility, where blame is shifted onto others or external circumstances. This evasion of accountability can create a cycle of defensiveness and emotional reactivity, hindering personal growth and damaging relationships.

By accepting responsibility for past mistakes, individuals can break this cycle. It involves a willingness to look inward and confront uncomfortable truths about one's behavior. This introspection is vital for fostering a sense of humility and understanding the impact of one's actions on others. This process can be facilitated through various practices, including mindfulness, journaling, and therapeutic interventions.

Steps to Embrace Accountability

1. Self-Reflection: Begin by engaging in self-reflection. This can involve journaling about specific incidents where you may have hurt others or failed to meet your own standards. Reflecting on these experiences helps to clarify the feelings associated with those events and can illuminate patterns of behavior that need to change.

2. Acknowledge Feelings: Recognizing the emotions tied to past mistakes—such as shame, guilt, or regret—is crucial. Allow yourself to feel these emotions without judgment. Understanding that these feelings are a natural part of the human experience can help mitigate the urge to dismiss or deny them.

3. Seek Feedback: Inviting trusted friends or family members to share their perspectives can provide valuable insights. This feedback can help you understand how your actions have affected others and can guide you in making amends.

4. Apologize and Make Amends: Once you've acknowledged your mistakes, the next step involves offering genuine apologies to those you've hurt. A sincere apology should convey understanding of the impact of your actions and express a commitment to change. Additionally, consider how you can make amends, whether through small acts of kindness or by actively working to change your behavior.

5. Learn from Mistakes: Instead of viewing mistakes as failures, reframe them as opportunities for learning and growth. Analyze what led to the mistake and identify strategies to prevent similar occurrences in the future. This proactive approach not only fosters personal development but also reinforces a commitment to accountability.

6. Cultivate Self-Compassion: Taking responsibility does not mean dwelling on guilt or self-blame. It's essential to practice self-compassion, recognizing that everyone makes mistakes. Allow yourself the grace to learn and grow from these experiences rather than letting them define you.

Building a Future of Integrity
By taking responsibility for past mistakes, individuals can lay the groundwork for a more authentic and empathetic life. This journey requires courage and vulnerability, but it ultimately leads to deeper connections with others and a stronger sense of self. Embracing accountability fosters trust in relationships, as others see your commitment to growth and integrity.

In conclusion, taking responsibility for past mistakes is a transformative process that involves self-reflection, acknowledgment of feelings, and a commitment to change. By approaching this journey with compassion and a willingness to learn, individuals can rebuild their lives and relationships, fostering a deeper sense of fulfillment and connection in their interactions with others.

How to Set and Achieve Personal Goals Without Narcissism
Setting and achieving personal goals is a fundamental aspect of personal development and self-improvement. However, for individuals with narcissistic tendencies, goal-setting can often be distorted by a need for external validation, competition, and self-centered motivations. To cultivate a healthier approach to goal-setting that promotes genuine growth and fulfillment, it is essential to focus on intrinsic motivations and self-awareness. Here are key strategies to set and achieve personal goals without falling into narcissistic patterns.

1. Establish Intrinsic Motivations
Rather than setting goals based on external validation—such as accolades, recognition, or social media approval—focus on intrinsic motivations. Ask yourself why you want to accomplish a specific goal. Is it to improve your skills, contribute to your community, or enhance your well-being? Defining your "why" helps to create goals that resonate with your values and passions rather than those imposed by societal expectations.

2. Set Realistic and Measurable Goals
To avoid the pitfalls of grandiosity often associated with narcissism, ensure that your goals are realistic and measurable. Employ the SMART criteria—Specific, Measurable, Achievable, Relevant, and Time-bound. This framework encourages practicality and clarity, allowing you to

track your progress and celebrate small victories along the way. For instance, instead of setting a vague goal of "getting fit," articulate it as "exercising for 30 minutes, five times a week for the next three months."

3. Practice Humility
Humility plays a crucial role in achieving goals without narcissism. Practice acknowledging your limitations and recognizing that growth is a process that often involves setbacks. Embrace the idea that it's okay to ask for help or seek feedback from others. This approach not only fosters personal growth but also enhances your relationships, allowing for collaboration and support rather than competition.

4. Emphasize Personal Growth Over Comparison
A common trap for those with narcissistic tendencies is comparing their achievements to others. To combat this, focus on your growth journey rather than how your achievements stack up against others. Keep a journal to reflect on your progress and the skills you have developed. Celebrate your unique path and recognize that every individual has their timeline for growth and success.

5. Create Accountability
Accountability can be instrumental in maintaining focus on your goals without succumbing to narcissistic impulses. Share your goals with trusted friends or family members who can provide support and constructive feedback. Consider forming an accountability group where you can discuss progress, challenges, and strategies with others. This communal approach not only encourages motivation but also fosters a sense of belonging and support.

6. Balance Self-Care and Ambition
While ambition is important, it must be balanced with self-care to prevent burnout and maintain emotional stability. Set aside time for self-care activities that rejuvenate you, whether that be exercise, meditation, or pursuing hobbies that bring you joy. A balanced approach allows for sustained motivation and encourages a holistic view of success that encompasses well-being.

7. Reflect and Adjust Goals
Regularly reflect on your goals and the motivations behind them. Allow yourself the flexibility to adjust your goals as you grow and change. This practice not only keeps you aligned with your values but also ensures that your goals remain relevant and fulfilling. Take the time to assess whether your goals continue to resonate with you or if they need recalibrating to fit your evolving self.

In conclusion, setting and achieving personal goals without narcissism requires a shift in focus from external validation to intrinsic motivation, humility, and personal growth. By employing these strategies, you can foster a healthier relationship with your aspirations, leading to a more fulfilling and authentic life.

Rebuilding Relationships with Integrity and Respect

Rebuilding relationships that have been strained or damaged by narcissistic tendencies is a challenging yet deeply rewarding endeavor. It requires a profound commitment to personal growth, empathy, and, most importantly, integrity and respect. Here, we explore the essential components of this process and provide actionable strategies for fostering healthier connections with others.

Understanding Integrity and Respect

Integrity involves being honest and having strong moral principles. It means being true to oneself and others, taking responsibility for past actions, and demonstrating consistency in one's values and behaviors. Respect, on the other hand, is about recognizing the inherent worth of others and valuing their feelings, opinions, and boundaries. Together, integrity and respect create a foundation for rebuilding trust and fostering healthy, reciprocal relationships.

Acknowledging Past Mistakes

The first step in rebuilding relationships is acknowledging the mistakes made. This requires a willingness to engage in self-reflection and an honest assessment of how one's actions may have affected others. Acknowledgment is not merely saying "I'm sorry"; it involves understanding the impact of one's behavior and accepting responsibility without deflecting blame or minimizing the hurt caused. This sincerity fosters an environment where healing can begin.

Practicing Active Listening

Active listening is a critical skill in rebuilding relationships. It goes beyond hearing words; it involves fully engaging with the speaker, reflecting on their emotions, and showing genuine interest in their perspective. Practicing active listening communicates respect and validates the other person's experiences. This practice can significantly enhance mutual understanding and lay the groundwork for deeper connections.

Setting Healthy Boundaries

Healthy boundaries are essential for any relationship. They protect individual autonomy while fostering an environment of respect. When rebuilding relationships, it's crucial to establish and communicate clear boundaries that honor both parties' needs. This includes respecting others' emotional spaces, being mindful of triggers, and being open to discussing personal limits. When both individuals feel safe and respected, relationships can flourish.

Rebuilding Trust through Consistency
Trust is the cornerstone of any relationship, and it takes time to rebuild once it has been compromised. Consistency in actions and words is vital. Demonstrating that you can be relied upon and that you respect the boundaries and feelings of others fosters an atmosphere of safety and trust. Small, consistent actions over time can help mend the fractures in a relationship and show a genuine commitment to change.

Cultivating Empathy
Empathy is the ability to understand and share the feelings of another. To rebuild relationships effectively, individuals must work on recognizing and addressing their empathy deficits. This involves not only acknowledging the emotions of others but also making an effort to feel and understand their experiences. Techniques such as perspective-taking, where one consciously tries to see things from another person's viewpoint, can enhance empathetic responses and deepen connections.

Open Communication
Effective communication is essential in any relationship, particularly when rebuilding after past conflicts. Being open about intentions, feelings, and expectations fosters transparency. Encouraging honest dialogue invites the other person to express their feelings and concerns, creating an inclusive environment for healing. It is important to approach these conversations with a mindset of curiosity rather than defensiveness, allowing for a constructive exchange.

Commitment to Personal Growth
Rebuilding relationships is not solely about repairing the past; it is also about committing to ongoing personal growth. This includes being open to feedback, continuously reflecting on one's actions, and seeking opportunities for self-improvement. When both individuals prioritize growth, the relationship can evolve into a healthier dynamic, characterized by mutual respect and integrity.

Conclusion
Rebuilding relationships with integrity and respect is a multifaceted process that requires dedication and effort. By acknowledging past mistakes, practicing active listening, establishing healthy boundaries, and fostering empathy, individuals can create a supportive environment for healing. With commitment and a focus on personal growth, it is possible to cultivate authentic, lasting connections that thrive on mutual respect and understanding.

Living a More Authentic, Empathetic Life

Living authentically and empathetically is essential for emotional well-being and interpersonal relationships. The journey toward authenticity begins with self-awareness and understanding one's values, beliefs, and desires. Authenticity requires individuals to embrace their true selves rather than conforming to societal expectations or external validations, which are often at the core of narcissistic tendencies.

Embracing Authenticity

To live authentically, one must engage in self-reflection and introspection. This involves examining personal values and motivations, identifying what truly matters in life, and recognizing the influences that may have led to inauthentic behaviors. Practicing mindfulness can be a valuable tool in this process, as it encourages individuals to remain present and aware of their thoughts and feelings without judgment. Journaling, meditation, or simply spending quiet time alone can help clarify one's identity and aspirations.

Moreover, authenticity encourages vulnerability. It's important to recognize that revealing one's true self, including imperfections and insecurities, fosters deeper connections with others. By sharing authentic experiences and feelings, individuals invite empathy and understanding, which can lead to stronger, more meaningful relationships.

Cultivating Empathy

Empathy is the ability to understand and share the feelings of others, and it plays a crucial role in fostering compassion and connection. To cultivate empathy, one can practice active listening—truly paying attention to what others are saying without planning a response while they speak. This not only allows for a better understanding of others' perspectives but also demonstrates respect and validation of their experiences.

Additionally, engaging in perspective-taking exercises can enhance empathy. This may involve imagining oneself in another person's situation or reflecting on how one would feel if faced with similar challenges. Such practices can deepen emotional connections and encourage a sense of community and belonging.

Further, volunteering and serving others can provide opportunities to connect with different individuals from various backgrounds. By understanding their struggles and triumphs, one can develop a broader perspective on life and cultivate a more profound sense of compassion.

The Role of Gratitude

Gratitude is a powerful antidote to narcissism and self-centeredness. By regularly acknowledging and appreciating the positive aspects of life, individuals can shift their focus away from themselves and their needs. This practice encourages a more balanced perspective, where the happiness and achievements of others are celebrated, fostering a sense of interconnectedness.

Creating a daily gratitude practice, such as keeping a gratitude journal or sharing moments of appreciation with loved ones, can reinforce this mindset. Over time, expressing gratitude becomes an ingrained habit that contributes to a more fulfilling and empathetic life.

Building Authentic Connections
Building authentic, empathetic relationships requires effort and commitment. It involves being open and honest in communication, setting healthy boundaries, and being willing to engage in difficult conversations when necessary. Relationships flourish when both parties feel valued and understood, which can only occur in an environment of trust and respect.

Moreover, it's important to surround oneself with individuals who also prioritize authenticity and empathy. Building a supportive community encourages growth and nurtures a culture of understanding. Engaging with like-minded individuals fosters an environment where everyone can thrive, ultimately leading to a more fulfilling and purpose-driven life.

Conclusion
Living a more authentic, empathetic life is a transformative journey that fosters personal growth and enriches relationships. By embracing authenticity, cultivating empathy, practicing gratitude, and building genuine connections, individuals can break free from narcissistic patterns and contribute positively to the world around them. This journey not only enhances one's own life but also creates a ripple effect, fostering a more compassionate and understanding society.

Chapter 18

The Role of Therapy in Healing Narcissism

Finding the Right Therapist for Narcissistic Traits
When embarking on the journey of healing from narcissistic traits, one of the most crucial steps is finding the right therapist. The therapeutic relationship can provide the support, guidance, and tools necessary for personal growth and change. However, not all therapists are equipped to address the complexities associated with narcissism. Here are key considerations to help you find a therapist who can effectively assist you in this transformative process.

Understanding Narcissistic Traits
Before seeking therapy, it's important to understand what narcissistic traits entail. Narcissism can manifest in various ways, including an inflated sense of self-importance, a constant need for admiration, and difficulties with empathy. These traits can stem from deep-seated insecurities and emotional wounds, making it essential to find a therapist who is knowledgeable about narcissism and its psychological underpinnings. A therapist with experience in this area will be better equipped to help you navigate your specific challenges.

Look for Specialized Training
When searching for a therapist, consider those who have specialized training in personality disorders, particularly Narcissistic Personality Disorder (NPD). Therapists who have pursued further education or certifications in this realm are likely to possess a deeper understanding of the dynamics at play. You can inquire about their experience with narcissism during an initial consultation or through research on their professional background.

Assessing Therapeutic Approaches
Different therapeutic modalities can be effective in addressing narcissistic traits. Cognitive Behavioral Therapy (CBT) is often beneficial as it helps individuals recognize and reframe negative thought patterns. Additionally, Dialectical Behavior Therapy (DBT) can be useful in enhancing emotional regulation and interpersonal effectiveness. Psychodynamic therapy, which focuses on exploring underlying emotions and historical context, can also be valuable for those with narcissistic traits. Understanding the therapist's approach and ensuring it aligns with your needs is vital.

Building a Therapeutic Alliance
A strong therapeutic alliance is foundational for successful therapy. You should feel

comfortable, understood, and respected by your therapist. This relationship can be challenging for individuals with narcissistic traits, as issues related to vulnerability and trust may arise. During initial sessions, pay attention to how the therapist responds to your concerns and whether they create a safe space for exploration. A therapist who demonstrates empathy, patience, and a non-judgmental attitude can help foster this alliance.

Exploring Experience with Empathy Development
One key area for growth for individuals struggling with narcissism is the development of empathy. Ask potential therapists about their experience and strategies for fostering empathy in clients. Effective therapists will have tools and techniques to help you recognize and improve your empathetic responses, which is fundamental to healing and building healthier relationships.

Checking Credentials and Reviews
It's also essential to verify the therapist's credentials. Look for licensed practitioners, such as psychologists, licensed clinical social workers, or licensed professional counselors. Additionally, check online reviews or ask for referrals to gauge their effectiveness and approachability from previous clients. This feedback can provide valuable insights into their therapeutic style and the experiences of others.

Commitment to the Process
Finally, healing from narcissistic traits is a long-term commitment. Ensure that the therapist you choose is dedicated to working with clients over time to facilitate meaningful change. Discuss the expected course of therapy and their approach to measuring progress. A therapist's commitment to your growth can significantly impact your journey toward healing.

In conclusion, finding the right therapist for narcissistic traits requires careful consideration of their expertise, approach, and ability to form a supportive therapeutic alliance. Taking the time to choose the right professional can lead to profound personal growth, healthier relationships, and a more fulfilling life free from the constraints of narcissism.

The Benefits of Cognitive Behavioral Therapy for Narcissism
Cognitive Behavioral Therapy (CBT) is a widely recognized and effective therapeutic approach for a variety of psychological issues, including narcissistic traits and behaviors. While individuals with narcissistic tendencies may initially resist the idea of therapy, CBT offers valuable tools and techniques that can lead to significant personal growth and healing. Here are several key benefits of CBT for those struggling with narcissism.

1. Challenging Distorted Thinking Patterns
One of the core features of narcissism is the presence of distorted thinking patterns, such as grandiosity, entitlement, or a pervasive need for admiration. CBT helps individuals identify and challenge these cognitive distortions. Through structured sessions, clients learn to recognize negative thought patterns and replace them with more balanced and realistic perspectives. For example, rather than thinking, "I am superior to everyone else," a client might learn to think, "I have strengths, but so do others." This shift in thinking can reduce feelings of superiority and increase empathy towards others.

2. Enhancing Self-Awareness
Self-awareness is a crucial component for personal growth, particularly for individuals with narcissistic traits. CBT encourages clients to engage in self-reflection and mindfulness, which increases awareness of their thoughts, feelings, and behaviors. By understanding how their actions affect others and recognizing their emotional responses, clients can begin to develop a more nuanced understanding of themselves. This self-awareness is essential for breaking the cycle of self-centeredness that often characterizes narcissism.

3. Building Emotional Regulation Skills
Many individuals with narcissistic traits struggle with emotional regulation, leading to intense reactions to criticism or perceived slights. CBT teaches practical skills for managing emotions effectively. Techniques such as mindfulness, breathing exercises, and cognitive restructuring help individuals learn to respond to emotional triggers in healthier ways. For instance, rather than reacting defensively when faced with criticism, they can practice pausing, reflecting, and responding thoughtfully. This emotional resilience fosters healthier relationships and improves overall well-being.

4. Developing Empathy
A significant challenge for those with narcissistic traits is a deficit in empathy, which can hinder their relationships. CBT can facilitate the development of empathy by helping clients understand the emotions and perspectives of others. Through exercises that encourage perspective-taking and role-playing, clients can learn to recognize and validate the feelings of those around them. This practice not only enhances interpersonal relationships but also contributes to a deeper sense of connection and belonging.

5. Focusing on Personal Accountability
Narcissism often involves a lack of accountability for one's actions and an externalization of blame. CBT places a strong emphasis on personal responsibility, encouraging clients to examine their role in their relationships and interactions. By fostering a mindset that values

accountability, clients can work towards repairing damaged relationships and building trust with others. This process often includes setting personal goals and taking actionable steps towards positive change.

6. Creating Lasting Change
CBT is structured and goal-oriented, making it an effective approach for instilling lasting change in behavior and thought patterns. Clients are encouraged to practice the skills learned in therapy outside of sessions, reinforcing healthier habits over time. The skills acquired through CBT can lead to improved self-esteem, enhanced relationships, and a more fulfilling life devoid of narcissistic tendencies.

In conclusion, Cognitive Behavioral Therapy offers a robust framework for individuals struggling with narcissism. By addressing distorted thinking, enhancing self-awareness, building emotional regulation skills, developing empathy, fostering personal accountability, and facilitating lasting change, CBT provides a pathway to healing. Individuals willing to engage in this transformative process can experience profound shifts in their lives, relationships, and overall mental health.

How Group Therapy Can Help Build Empathy and Connection
Group therapy is an increasingly recognized and effective therapeutic approach for individuals grappling with narcissistic traits and behaviors. This form of therapy provides a unique environment that fosters empathy and connection, which are often lacking in individuals with narcissistic tendencies. Here, we explore the mechanisms through which group therapy can facilitate these essential emotional skills.

Shared Experiences and Understanding
One of the most powerful aspects of group therapy is the shared experience among participants. Individuals who enter group therapy typically carry similar struggles, such as feelings of isolation, inadequacy, or the need for constant validation. As participants share their stories and feelings, they are often surprised to discover that others have faced similar challenges. This recognition helps to diminish feelings of isolation and fosters a sense of belonging.

Moreover, hearing others articulate their experiences can create a mirror effect, allowing group members to reflect on their own behaviors and emotions. This process of self-reflection is crucial for individuals with narcissistic tendencies, who often lack insight into how their actions affect others. By listening to diverse perspectives within a supportive group, participants can begin to understand the impact of their behaviors, enhancing their empathy for others.

Developing Emotional Intelligence

Group therapy sessions often involve discussions about emotions, vulnerabilities, and interpersonal dynamics. This setting encourages participants to express their feelings openly, which can be particularly challenging for those with narcissistic traits, who may fear vulnerability. As participants practice articulating their feelings and reactions in a safe space, they enhance their emotional intelligence.

Emotional intelligence is the ability to recognize, understand, and manage our own emotions and those of others. For individuals with narcissistic behaviors, developing this skill is essential for fostering genuine connections. Group therapy provides opportunities to practice empathy through active listening and validating others' experiences, which contributes to a deeper understanding of the emotional landscapes of their peers.

Feedback and Accountability

In group therapy, feedback is a critical component of the healing process. Participants are encouraged to provide constructive feedback to one another, which can be a powerful tool for personal growth. For those with narcissistic traits, receiving honest feedback can initially be challenging, as it may feel like a threat to their self-image. However, when delivered in a supportive environment, this feedback can encourage self-examination and accountability.

By learning to accept and integrate feedback, individuals can gain insights into their behaviors that may have previously gone unexamined. This accountability fosters a sense of responsibility towards others, which is fundamental in building empathy. Participants learn that their actions have consequences, not just for themselves but also for those around them.

Building Trust and Authentic Connections

Group therapy is inherently about connection. As participants engage in discussions and share their vulnerabilities, trust begins to develop within the group. This trust is essential for cultivating authentic relationships, something that individuals with narcissistic traits often struggle to achieve due to their self-centered focus.

Through repeated interactions, participants learn the value of mutual support and the importance of being present for others. This shift from self-focus to other-focus is a significant step in healing narcissistic tendencies. The compassion and understanding that flourish within the group can serve as a model for how to engage in relationships outside of the therapeutic setting.

Conclusion

Group therapy offers a multifaceted approach to building empathy and connection for individuals struggling with narcissism. By providing a space for shared experiences, enhancing emotional intelligence, fostering accountability, and building trust, group therapy can help participants transform their relationships with themselves and others. Ultimately, this journey towards empathy and connection is essential not only for personal growth but also for cultivating healthier, more fulfilling relationships in all areas of life.

Self-Help Books and Resources for Narcissism Recovery

The journey toward understanding and overcoming narcissistic traits can be complex and often requires a multifaceted approach. Self-help books and resources play a pivotal role in this process. They provide individuals with insights, strategies, and tools to foster self-awareness, empathy, and personal growth. Below, we explore some highly regarded self-help books and additional resources that can support recovery from narcissism.

Key Self-Help Books

1. "Will I Ever Be Good Enough? Healing the Daughters of Narcissistic Mothers" by Karyl McBride

This book addresses the specific experiences of women raised by narcissistic mothers. McBride offers practical advice and therapeutic techniques that help readers understand the impact of their upbringing on their self-esteem and relationships. The book emphasizes the importance of self-compassion and reclamation of one's identity.

2. "The Narcissist You Know: Defending Yourself Against Extreme Narcissists in an All-About-Me Age" by Joseph Burgo

Burgo's work delves into the various manifestations of narcissism in everyday life and offers insights on how to recognize these behaviors in oneself and others. The book provides practical strategies for dealing with narcissistic individuals and fosters an understanding of how to cultivate healthier relationships.

3. "Self-Compassion: The Proven Power of Being Kind to Yourself" by Kristin Neff

While not exclusively about narcissism, Neff's book emphasizes the importance of self-compassion as an antidote to the shame and guilt often associated with narcissistic traits. It offers exercises and guided meditations that can help individuals shift their focus from self-criticism to self-kindness, an essential step in healing.

4. "The Drama of the Gifted Child: The Search for the True Self" by Alice Miller

This classic work explores how childhood experiences, particularly in families with narcissistic parents, can lead to the development of narcissistic traits in adulthood. Miller encourages readers to confront their past and embrace their true selves, paving the way for healing and personal authenticity.

5. "Rethinking Narcissism: The Bad—and Surprising Good—About Feeling Special" by Craig Malkin

Malkin offers a nuanced perspective on narcissism, distinguishing between healthy and unhealthy forms. His book encourages readers to embrace the positive aspects of self-importance while managing the detrimental effects of extreme narcissism. He provides practical tools for self-assessment and growth.

Online Resources and Support Groups

In addition to books, various online resources can support individuals on their journey:

- **Podcasts and Webinars:** Many mental health professionals share insights on narcissism through podcasts and webinars, providing valuable discussions and expert advice. Platforms like iTunes and Spotify feature a range of shows focusing on narcissism and personal development.

- **Online Support Groups:** Websites like Reddit and specialized forums offer community support for individuals dealing with narcissistic traits or relationships. Engaging with others who share similar experiences can provide validation and encouragement.

- **Therapy Apps:** Apps such as BetterHelp or Talkspace connect users with licensed therapists specializing in personality disorders and related issues. These platforms can provide immediate access to professional guidance from the comfort of home.

Conclusion

Starting the path to recovery from narcissistic traits is a courageous and transformative journey. Self-help books and resources provide essential tools for understanding the complexities of narcissism, fostering self-compassion, and cultivating healthier relationships. By integrating the insights gained from these resources with active self-reflection and possibly professional guidance, individuals can navigate their healing journey more effectively, ultimately leading to a more authentic and fulfilling life.

The Long-Term Commitment to Healing and Growth

Healing from narcissistic traits and behaviors is a profound journey that requires a long-term commitment to personal growth. Unlike a quick fix, this process involves a deep, ongoing transformation that can significantly enhance one's emotional well-being, relationships, and overall life satisfaction. It is important to understand that this commitment is not merely a phase but a continuous practice that fosters resilience and self-awareness.

Embracing Change

The first step in this long-term commitment is embracing the need for change. Many individuals with narcissistic traits might initially resist the idea that they need to change, often due to defensiveness or denial. Acknowledging that these traits stem from deeper emotional wounds is crucial. This recognition creates a foundation for healing, as it allows individuals to confront the underlying issues that have contributed to their narcissism, such as insecurity, fear of rejection, or a need for external validation.

The Role of Self-Reflection

Self-reflection is an essential component of this commitment. Regularly engaging in self-reflection—whether through journaling, meditation, or therapy—enables individuals to critically assess their behaviors and thoughts. This practice helps to identify patterns and triggers that lead to narcissistic responses, allowing individuals to develop healthier coping mechanisms. By fostering a habit of introspection, individuals can cultivate a greater understanding of their motivations and emotional responses, which is vital for sustained growth.

Setting Realistic Goals

Establishing realistic and achievable goals is another critical aspect of committing to long-term healing. These goals should focus not only on reducing narcissistic behaviors but also on enhancing other areas of life, such as emotional intelligence, empathy, and relationship skills. For instance, a person might set a goal to practice active listening in conversations or to express gratitude daily. Achieving small, incremental goals can lead to substantial changes over time, reinforcing the belief that growth is possible and ongoing.

Seeking Support

Another vital element of this journey is seeking support, whether through professional therapy, support groups, or trusted friends and family. Engaging with a therapist who understands the complexities of narcissism can provide invaluable insights and tools for navigating the healing process. Group therapy can also create a safe space for sharing experiences and learning from others who are on a similar path. Building a support network fosters accountability, encouragement, and understanding, which are essential for long-term success.

Cultivating Resilience and Patience
Healing from narcissistic traits requires resilience and patience. Setbacks are a natural part of the healing process, and it is essential to approach them with self-compassion rather than self-criticism. Recognizing that growth is a non-linear journey can help individuals remain motivated and committed, even when faced with challenges. Cultivating patience allows for a deeper understanding of oneself and the complexities of human behavior, ultimately leading to more profound transformations.

Celebrating Progress
Finally, regularly celebrating progress—no matter how small—is crucial in maintaining motivation and commitment to healing. Acknowledging improvements in emotional awareness, empathy, and relationship dynamics reinforces the positive changes that are taking place. This practice not only boosts self-esteem but also encourages continued growth and development.

In conclusion, the long-term commitment to healing and growth from narcissistic traits is a multifaceted process that encompasses self-reflection, goal-setting, seeking support, resilience, and celebrating progress. By understanding that this journey is ongoing and requires dedication, individuals can move toward a more authentic, empathetic, and fulfilling life. Embracing this commitment can lead to profound changes not only within oneself but also in one's relationships and overall quality of life.

Chapter 19

Success Without Narcissism

Redefining Success in Your Life

In a world often dominated by social metrics—likes, shares, accolades, and material wealth—it's crucial to redefine what success truly means to you. For many, the conventional definitions of success are closely tied to external validation, which can foster narcissistic tendencies and lead to an unfulfilled life. Moving away from this notion involves a profound shift in mindset, focusing instead on intrinsic values that promote genuine happiness and self-acceptance.

The Detriments of External Validation

External validation refers to the approval or recognition we seek from others to feel worthy or successful. This can manifest through social media likes, professional accolades, or societal status. While a certain degree of acknowledgment is natural and can be affirming, relying on it as a primary measure of success can lead to a precarious existence. The pursuit of external validation often breeds a cycle of dependency, where self-worth becomes contingent upon others' opinions. This can result in feelings of inadequacy, anxiety, and even depression when such validation is absent or fleeting.

Identifying Your Core Values

To redefine success, begin by identifying your core values. What genuinely matters to you? Is it creativity, integrity, kindness, family, or personal growth? Reflecting on these values can guide your understanding of success. Engage in activities like journaling, meditation, or deep conversations with trusted friends to explore what brings you joy and fulfillment. By anchoring your definition of success in your values, you can create a more stable foundation for your self-esteem.

Setting Personal Goals

Once you have a clear understanding of your values, translate them into personal goals that resonate with your authentic self. Unlike traditional success metrics, these goals should focus on internal growth rather than societal expectations. For instance, if creativity is a core value, set a goal to complete a personal project, like writing a book or painting. If connection is important, aim to deepen relationships with friends and family. By aligning your goals with your values, you cultivate a sense of accomplishment that is intrinsically rewarding.

Embracing the Journey
Redefining success also involves embracing the journey rather than fixating solely on outcomes. This perspective shift allows you to appreciate the learning process, the skills you develop, and the resilience you build along the way. Celebrate small victories and acknowledge the effort you put into your endeavors, irrespective of external recognition. Adopting a growth mindset can facilitate this process, encouraging you to view challenges as opportunities for development rather than threats to your self-worth.

Cultivating Gratitude
Gratitude is a powerful tool in shifting your focus from external validation to internal fulfillment. Regularly practicing gratitude can help you appreciate what you have rather than what society dictates you should achieve. Consider maintaining a gratitude journal where you list things you are thankful for daily. This practice fosters a deeper appreciation for life's simple pleasures and reinforces the idea that success can be found in everyday moments, relationships, and experiences.

Finding Fulfillment in Helping Others
Lastly, consider redefining success by contributing to the well-being of others. Engaging in acts of kindness or community service can cultivate a sense of purpose that transcends personal achievement. By focusing on how you can impact the lives of those around you, you shift your attention from self-centered pursuits to a broader, more fulfilling definition of success. This not only enhances your own well-being but also fosters genuine connections with others, reinforcing the idea that success is best measured through empathy and service.

Conclusion
In conclusion, redefining success involves a conscious effort to move away from external validation and embrace an intrinsic approach focused on personal values, goals, growth, and connection. By doing so, you can cultivate a more authentic and fulfilling life, one that celebrates who you are rather than how you're perceived by others. Embrace this journey, and you may find that success is not a destination but a continuous process of self-discovery and genuine connection with the world around you.

Developing a Healthy Work-Life Balance
Achieving a healthy work-life balance is essential for overall well-being and can significantly impact your mental health, relationships, and productivity. In the context of overcoming narcissistic tendencies, a balanced approach to work and life can help mitigate self-centered behaviors and foster a sense of community and empathy. Here, we will explore practical strategies to cultivate a work-life balance that supports personal growth, emotional health, and

relational integrity.

1. Setting Clear Boundaries
Establishing clear boundaries between work and personal life is foundational to achieving a healthy balance. This can involve setting specific work hours and adhering to them, ensuring that work does not encroach into personal time. Communicate these boundaries to colleagues and supervisors to foster a culture of respect for personal time. For example, resist the urge to check work emails after hours or during weekends, creating a designated space for focused work that is separate from your living area.

2. Prioritizing Self-Care
Self-care is crucial in maintaining a balanced lifestyle, especially for individuals recovering from narcissistic traits. Engage in activities that promote relaxation and rejuvenation, such as exercise, meditation, or hobbies that bring joy and fulfillment. Regularly scheduled self-care activities can serve as a reminder that your well-being is important and help counteract the need for constant external validation that often accompanies narcissism. Incorporating self-care into your routine fosters a sense of self-worth that does not rely solely on work achievements.

3. Time Management Techniques
Effective time management is vital for achieving a work-life balance. Utilize techniques such as prioritization and scheduling to ensure that you allocate sufficient time for both work responsibilities and personal activities. The Eisenhower Matrix, for instance, can help you distinguish between urgent and important tasks, allowing you to focus on what truly matters. By managing your time effectively, you can minimize the stress that often leads to neglecting personal relationships and self-care.

4. Learning to Say No
For someone struggling with narcissistic tendencies, the pressure to overcommit can be overwhelming. It's essential to recognize that saying "no" to additional responsibilities, whether at work or in personal life, is a necessary step toward maintaining balance. This not only prevents burnout but also allows you to dedicate quality time to the relationships and activities that genuinely matter to you. Practicing assertiveness in this manner fosters a sense of control and diminishes the fear of disappointing others that often drives narcissistic behavior.

5. Embracing Flexibility
Flexibility in both work and personal life can significantly enhance your ability to maintain balance. This might include negotiating remote work options or flexible hours that allow you to manage personal commitments without sacrificing productivity. Embracing flexibility can help

alleviate the rigid thinking patterns often associated with narcissism, promoting a more adaptable mindset that values both work and personal relationships.

6. Cultivating Connections

Building strong relationships outside of work is vital for emotional health and can counteract the isolating tendencies of narcissism. Dedicate time to nurture friendships and family relationships, ensuring that your social life is rich and fulfilling. Engaging in community service or group activities can also enhance your sense of connection and empathy, helping to ground you in the importance of relationships beyond your professional identity.

7. Reflecting Regularly

Finally, regular self-reflection is key to maintaining a healthy work-life balance. Take time to evaluate how well you are integrating work and personal life. Journaling can be an effective method for tracking your feelings, identifying stressors, and celebrating your achievements outside of work. This practice not only fosters self-awareness but also reinforces the idea that your value extends beyond professional success.

In conclusion, developing a healthy work-life balance is an ongoing process that requires intention and commitment. By setting boundaries, prioritizing self-care, mastering time management, learning to say no, embracing flexibility, cultivating connections, and reflecting regularly, you can create a fulfilling life that nurtures both your professional aspirations and personal well-being. This balance is essential for fostering empathy, understanding, and authentic relationships, ultimately leading to a more profound and lasting transformation away from narcissistic tendencies.

Finding Fulfillment in Helping Others

In the journey towards overcoming narcissistic tendencies, finding fulfillment in helping others emerges as a transformative and pivotal practice. This section explores the profound impact of altruism on personal growth, the psychological benefits of serving others, and practical ways to cultivate a mindset focused on contributions rather than self-centeredness.

The Psychological Shift

At its core, narcissism often stems from a deep-seated need for validation and external approval. Individuals with narcissistic traits may become preoccupied with their accomplishments, status, and image, leading to a cycle of emptiness and dissatisfaction. In contrast, when individuals shift their focus from themselves to the well-being of others, they open the door to a more profound sense of purpose and fulfillment. Helping others fosters a sense of belonging and connection, crucial elements for emotional and psychological well-being.

Research has shown that engaging in altruistic behavior can lead to what is often referred to as the "helper's high," a state of euphoria and satisfaction that arises from acts of kindness. This positive emotional state can counteract feelings of shame, guilt, and insecurity that often accompany narcissistic behaviors. By actively participating in the well-being of others, individuals can experience an increase in self-worth that is not reliant on external validation.

Building Connections Through Service
Helping others creates opportunities for building genuine relationships grounded in empathy and mutual respect. Unlike the superficial connections often associated with narcissistic interactions, altruistic efforts foster deeper emotional bonds. When individuals engage in volunteer work, community service, or even small acts of kindness, they not only contribute positively to their communities but also cultivate authentic relationships with those they help.

Moreover, these interactions provide individuals with valuable perspectives. By listening to the stories and struggles of others, individuals can gain insights into the human experience, which can enhance their empathy and understanding. This shift from self-focused narratives to shared experiences is crucial for healing and personal growth.

Practical Ways to Help Others

1. Volunteering: Engaging in volunteer work is one of the most impactful ways to help others. Whether it's serving at a local shelter, participating in environmental clean-ups, or mentoring youth, volunteering offers a tangible way to make a difference. It allows individuals to step outside of their own lives and contribute to the greater good.

2. Acts of Kindness: Incorporating small acts of kindness into daily routines can also foster fulfillment. This might include helping a neighbor with groceries, offering to listen to a friend in need, or simply expressing gratitude. These moments not only uplift others but also reinforce a sense of community and connection.

3. Sharing Skills: Consider what unique skills or knowledge you possess that could benefit others. Teaching a class, offering free consultations, or sharing your expertise in community workshops can empower others while providing you with a sense of accomplishment and purpose.

4. Listening: Sometimes, the most profound way to help is by simply being present. Active listening, where one fully engages with another person's thoughts and feelings, can provide immense support. This practice not only aids those who may feel unheard but also reinforces the listener's emotional intelligence and empathy.

5. Participating in Support Groups: Joining or forming support groups where individuals can share experiences and offer encouragement can be immensely beneficial. These groups foster a sense of community and shared understanding, which is particularly valuable for those navigating their own challenges.

Conclusion
Finding fulfillment in helping others is a powerful antidote to the emptiness that often accompanies narcissistic tendencies. By shifting focus from self to service, individuals can cultivate genuine connections, enhance their emotional well-being, and ultimately lead a more fulfilling life. Through acts of kindness, community engagement, and a commitment to empathy, one can break free from the confines of narcissism, embracing a life rich in purpose and connection.

Practicing Gratitude and Humility in Achievements
In a world that often equates success with self-promotion and external validation, cultivating gratitude and humility in the context of our achievements becomes crucial for personal growth and emotional well-being. This practice not only helps mitigate narcissistic tendencies but also fosters deeper connections with others and a more profound sense of fulfillment.

The Importance of Gratitude
Gratitude is a powerful emotional state that involves recognizing and appreciating the positive aspects of our lives, including our achievements. Practicing gratitude shifts our focus away from a self-centered view of success to a broader perspective that acknowledges the contributions of others and the circumstances that enabled our accomplishments.

1. Acknowledging Support: Often, our achievements are the result of collective efforts. Whether it's family, friends, teachers, or colleagues who have offered guidance, support, or encouragement, recognizing their roles fosters a sense of community and interconnectedness. By expressing gratitude for their contributions, we not only honor them but also reinforce our relationships.

2. Fostering Resilience: Gratitude helps build emotional resilience. When we appreciate what we have achieved, we can weather setbacks more effectively. Instead of viewing failures as reflections of our worth, gratitude allows us to see them as opportunities for growth and learning. This mindset encourages a healthier approach to challenges, reducing the likelihood of narcissistic defensiveness.

3. Enhancing Well-Being: Numerous studies indicate that practicing gratitude is linked to improved mental health. It can reduce feelings of envy, resentment, and frustration, which are often associated with narcissistic traits. By focusing on what we have rather than what we lack, we cultivate a more positive outlook that enhances overall well-being.

The Role of Humility

Humility is the ability to recognize our limitations and value others' contributions. It is a counterbalance to the self-aggrandizing tendencies of narcissism, promoting a balanced view of oneself.

1. Accepting Imperfection: Embracing humility involves acknowledging that no one is perfect, including ourselves. This acceptance allows us to celebrate our achievements without falling into the trap of superiority. Recognizing our imperfections can lead to a more authentic sense of self-worth, fostering genuine self-esteem based on who we are rather than what we accomplish.

2. Learning from Others: Humility opens the door to learning. When we admit that we don't have all the answers, we become more receptive to feedback and different perspectives. This willingness to learn from others can enrich our experiences and enhance our growth. It also cultivates respect and empathy, essential components for nurturing healthy relationships.

3. Promoting a Culture of Support: When we practice humility, we create an environment that encourages collaboration and support rather than competition. We recognize the value in others' achievements, which fosters a sense of camaraderie and mutual respect. This shift from a self-centered viewpoint to one that embraces collective success strengthens social bonds and creates a more positive atmosphere in both personal and professional settings.

Integrating Gratitude and Humility into Daily Life

1. Gratitude Journaling: Taking time each day to reflect on what you are grateful for can shift your perspective. Write down your achievements alongside the people or circumstances that contributed to them. This practice reinforces a sense of interconnectedness and appreciation.

2. Verbal Acknowledgment: Make it a habit to express gratitude to those who have supported you. Whether through a simple thank-you note or a heartfelt conversation, acknowledging their role fosters stronger relationships and reinforces humility.

3. Celebrate Others: Actively recognizing and celebrating the achievements of others, whether in your personal life or workplace, creates a culture of mutual respect and support. This practice can help diminish feelings of competition and resentment.

By integrating gratitude and humility into our understanding of achievements, we can move towards a more balanced life, free from the constraints of narcissism. These practices not only enhance our emotional health but also enrich our relationships, paving the way for a more fulfilling and connected existence.

Living a Life of Service and Contribution

Living a life of service and contribution is a powerful antidote to narcissism, fostering a sense of purpose and connection that transcends the self. This approach not only benefits others but also cultivates personal growth, empathy, and fulfillment. The following exploration delves into the importance of service, practical ways to contribute meaningfully, and the psychological benefits of adopting a service-oriented mindset.

The Importance of Service

At its core, a service-oriented life is about recognizing the interconnectedness of humanity. Narcissism often thrives on self-centeredness and the need for external validation, leading to isolation and dissatisfaction. In contrast, service encourages individuals to look beyond themselves, fostering a sense of belonging and community. When one engages in acts of kindness, whether small or large, it creates a ripple effect that enhances the social fabric and builds a supportive environment.

Moreover, serving others nurtures empathy. Engaging with diverse communities and understanding their challenges can help dismantle the barriers of self-absorption. Service also provides an opportunity to reflect on one's privileges and challenges, promoting gratitude and humility. This shift in perspective not only helps in mitigating narcissistic tendencies but also enriches the individual's life experience.

Practical Ways to Contribute

1. Volunteering: One of the most direct ways to engage in service is through volunteering. This could involve helping at local shelters, participating in community clean-up initiatives, or mentoring youth. Choose causes that resonate with you, as personal connection enhances the experience and commitment.

2. Acts of Kindness: Service doesn't always have to be grand. Simple acts of kindness—such as helping a neighbor, offering emotional support to a friend, or engaging in random acts of kindness—can make a significant difference. These small gestures can foster a sense of community and belonging.

3. Sharing Skills: Utilize your talents to help others. Whether through teaching, coaching, or offering pro bono services, sharing your skills not only contributes to others' growth but also reinforces your sense of purpose and self-worth.

4. Advocacy: Engage in advocacy for social justice, environmental issues, or mental health awareness. This can include raising awareness through social media, participating in community discussions, or supporting organizations that align with your values. Advocacy amplifies the voices of those who may feel unheard and contributes to systemic change.

5. Creating Community: Organize or participate in community events that bring people together. This could be anything from neighborhood potlucks to book clubs or support groups. Building connections fosters a sense of belonging and helps combat feelings of isolation often associated with narcissism.

Psychological Benefits of a Service-Oriented Life

Engaging in a life of service and contribution provides numerous psychological benefits. First, it can enhance overall well-being and life satisfaction. Studies have shown that individuals who engage in altruistic behavior report higher levels of happiness and fulfillment. This is largely due to the release of endorphins, often referred to as the "helper's high," which can boost mood and reduce stress.

Second, service can foster resilience. By focusing on the needs of others, individuals can gain perspective on their struggles, which can mitigate feelings of inadequacy and self-doubt. This shift in focus from self to others can help individuals cultivate a healthier self-esteem that does not rely on external validation.

Lastly, living a life of service encourages ongoing personal growth. It challenges individuals to step outside their comfort zones, confront biases, and develop new skills. This continuous learning and adaptation foster a mindset of growth rather than the stagnation associated with narcissistic behaviors.

In conclusion, embracing a life of service and contribution not only benefits those around us but also serves as a vital pathway to personal transformation. By shifting focus from self to others, individuals can cultivate empathy, resilience, and a profound sense of purpose, ultimately leading to a more fulfilling and interconnected life.

Chapter 20

Living a Fulfilling, Narcissism-Free Life

The Daily Practices for a Balanced, Narcissism-Free Life

Living a fulfilling life free from narcissistic tendencies requires consistent effort and a commitment to personal growth. This section outlines key daily practices that can help cultivate a balanced, narcissism-free lifestyle, emphasizing self-awareness, empathy, and community engagement.

1. Mindfulness and Presence

Mindfulness is an essential practice for reducing narcissistic tendencies. By focusing on the present moment, individuals can become more aware of their thoughts and feelings without judgment. Daily mindfulness exercises, such as meditation or deep-breathing techniques, can help individuals recognize their self-centered thoughts and redirect their focus to the environment and people around them. This practice encourages a sense of connection to others and fosters an appreciation for the present, reducing the urge for external validation.

2. Gratitude Journaling

Starting or ending each day with gratitude journaling can profoundly impact one's outlook on life. By writing down three to five things they are grateful for, individuals shift their focus from what they lack to what they have. This practice helps combat feelings of entitlement and fosters an appreciation for everyday blessings, from relationships to simple pleasures. Over time, gratitude journaling can rewire the brain to seek positivity rather than self-centeredness.

3. Acts of Kindness

Incorporating small acts of kindness into daily routines is a powerful way to move away from narcissism. This could include complimenting a co-worker, helping a neighbor, or volunteering time to assist those in need. Engaging in altruistic behaviors not only helps others but also cultivates empathy and a sense of connection to the community. Such actions can create a positive feedback loop, enhancing one's sense of self-worth through service rather than self-promotion.

4. Active Listening

Practicing active listening is crucial for building authentic relationships and fostering empathy. This involves fully focusing on the speaker, understanding their message, and responding thoughtfully. Individuals can set a daily intention to practice active listening in conversations, avoiding the urge to interrupt or redirect the focus to themselves. This practice enhances emotional connections and allows for deeper understanding, shifting the focus away from self-importance.

5. Self-Reflection
Regular self-reflection encourages individuals to examine their behaviors, motivations, and emotional responses. Setting aside time each day to reflect on interactions and personal feelings can help identify patterns of narcissistic thoughts and actions. Journaling about these reflections can facilitate deeper insights, leading to more mindful responses in the future. This practice not only promotes accountability but also encourages personal growth.

6. Setting Healthy Boundaries
Understanding and respecting personal boundaries is vital for healthy relationships. Daily practices should include assessing one's boundaries and ensuring they are communicated clearly to others. This involves both setting boundaries for oneself and respecting the boundaries of others, fostering mutual respect and understanding. Healthy boundaries help maintain a balanced sense of self-worth that is not dependent on external validation.

7. Engaging in Community
Participating in community activities fosters a sense of belonging and purpose that counters narcissistic tendencies. This could involve joining local clubs, participating in community service, or attending group gatherings. Engaging with others in shared activities promotes empathy and helps individuals appreciate diverse perspectives, moving away from self-centeredness.

Conclusion
Incorporating these daily practices into life can significantly diminish narcissistic tendencies and cultivate a deeper sense of fulfillment and connection with others. By focusing on mindfulness, gratitude, kindness, active listening, self-reflection, healthy boundaries, and community engagement, individuals can create a balanced, narcissism-free life. Ultimately, the journey toward personal growth and healthy relationships requires patience and commitment, but the rewards of living authentically and empathetically are profound.

Staying Grounded in Relationships
In the complex landscape of human interactions, staying grounded in relationships is essential for cultivating deep, meaningful connections. Emotional awareness and empathy serve as the foundation for healthy relationships, enabling individuals to navigate the intricacies of interpersonal dynamics while minimizing the risk of narcissistic tendencies. By developing these qualities, individuals can foster an environment of mutual respect and understanding, which is

crucial for sustaining long-lasting relationships.

Understanding Emotional Awareness

Emotional awareness is the ability to recognize and understand one's emotions as well as the emotions of others. This self-awareness provides insight into how feelings influence thoughts and behaviors. Being emotionally aware allows individuals to identify their emotional triggers, leading to healthier responses rather than reactive behaviors that can harm relationships.

To cultivate emotional awareness, one can engage in practices such as journaling and mindfulness meditation. Journaling encourages reflection on daily experiences and emotions, helping to identify patterns and triggers. Mindfulness, on the other hand, promotes being present in the moment and fully experiencing emotions without judgment. This practice can help individuals acknowledge their feelings and develop an understanding of how those feelings affect their relationships.

The Role of Empathy

Empathy is the ability to understand and share the feelings of another person. It is a vital component of emotional intelligence and serves as a bridge for connection in relationships. Empathy allows individuals to step into the shoes of others, offering compassion and understanding that can alleviate misunderstandings and conflicts.

There are two main types of empathy: cognitive and emotional. Cognitive empathy involves understanding another person's perspective and thoughts, while emotional empathy encompasses feeling what another person feels. Both forms are critical for developing a well-rounded empathetic approach in relationships.

To enhance empathy, one can practice active listening, which involves fully concentrating on the speaker, understanding their message, and responding thoughtfully. This technique not only validates the other person's feelings but also fosters a deeper emotional connection. Perspective-taking is another effective method; by imagining oneself in another's situation, individuals can broaden their understanding and appreciation of others' experiences.

Balancing Emotional Awareness and Empathy

While emotional awareness and empathy are powerful tools for relationship building, they must be balanced. Too much focus on one can lead to issues. For instance, excessive emotional awareness without empathy may result in self-centeredness, as individuals become overly focused on their feelings at the expense of recognizing others' emotions. Conversely, being highly empathetic without self-awareness can lead to emotional burnout, as individuals might absorb others' feelings and neglect their own emotional needs.

Practical Applications in Relationships
To stay grounded in relationships, individuals can implement practical strategies that integrate emotional awareness and empathy. Regular check-ins with oneself and others can facilitate open communication about feelings and needs. Establishing a routine for shared activities, such as family dinners or partner talks, can enhance emotional intimacy.

Setting boundaries is equally important. Recognizing when to engage and when to step back allows individuals to maintain emotional stability while fostering healthy relationships.

Conclusion
Staying grounded in relationships requires a commitment to emotional awareness and empathy. By cultivating these qualities, individuals can build a solid foundation for their connections, leading to deeper, more authentic relationships. As emotional awareness grows, so does the ability to empathize, creating a virtuous cycle that enriches personal connections. Ultimately, the journey toward emotional awareness and empathy is not merely about improving relationships but about fostering a more fulfilling, compassionate life.

How to Build Long-Lasting, Authentic Connections with Others
Building long-lasting, authentic connections with others is essential for emotional well-being and personal growth. Relationships built on authenticity foster trust, empathy, and mutual respect, serving as a foundation for a fulfilling life. However, achieving such connections requires intentional effort and self-awareness. Here are several strategies to help cultivate and maintain these meaningful relationships.

1. Practice Vulnerability
Vulnerability is the cornerstone of authentic relationships. It involves sharing your true thoughts, feelings, and experiences with others, which creates a deeper sense of connection. When you allow yourself to be vulnerable, you invite others to do the same, leading to mutual understanding and support. Start by sharing personal stories or expressing your feelings during conversations. This openness can strengthen bonds and encourage others to reciprocate, fostering a safe space for genuine connection.

2. Cultivate Empathy
Empathy is the ability to understand and share the feelings of others, and it plays a crucial role in building authentic connections. To cultivate empathy, practice active listening—give your full attention to the speaker, acknowledge their emotions, and respond thoughtfully. This not only

validates their feelings but also demonstrates that you genuinely care. Engaging in perspective-taking exercises can further enhance your empathetic skills, allowing you to appreciate others' viewpoints and experiences.

3. Communicate Openly and Honestly
Clear and honest communication is vital for nurturing authentic relationships. Share your thoughts and feelings openly, and encourage others to do the same. When discussing difficult topics, approach the conversation with kindness and respect. This transparency helps prevent misunderstandings and builds trust, as both parties feel comfortable expressing themselves without fear of judgment or retaliation.

4. Invest Time and Effort
Authentic connections require nurturing; therefore, investing time and effort into your relationships is essential. Regularly check in with friends and family, plan activities together, and be present in their lives. Prioritize quality time over quantity, focusing on meaningful interactions that reinforce your bond. Remember that building relationships takes time, so be patient and committed to the process.

5. Establish Healthy Boundaries
Healthy boundaries are crucial for maintaining authentic connections. They help protect your emotional well-being while allowing for mutual respect and understanding. Communicate your boundaries clearly and respectfully, and encourage others to express theirs. Recognizing and respecting the boundaries of others fosters an environment of trust and safety, allowing relationships to thrive.

6. Embrace Differences
Every individual is unique, and embracing these differences can enrich your relationships. Rather than seeking out people who are just like you, be open to connecting with those who have diverse perspectives and experiences. This diversity can lead to growth, learning, and deeper connections. Celebrate these differences and view them as opportunities for collaboration and understanding.

7. Practice Forgiveness
No relationship is immune to conflict or misunderstandings. Practicing forgiveness is crucial for maintaining long-lasting connections. Be willing to let go of grudges and approach conflicts with a mindset of understanding and reconciliation. This does not mean overlooking harmful behavior; rather, it involves recognizing mistakes, addressing concerns, and moving forward with compassion.

8. Celebrate Life Together
Sharing experiences and celebrating milestones together can fortify bonds. Whether it's a birthday, an accomplishment, or simply enjoying a beautiful day, take the time to acknowledge and celebrate these moments with those you care about. Such shared experiences create lasting memories and solidify your connection.

In conclusion, building long-lasting, authentic connections is a multifaceted process that requires effort, empathy, and commitment. By practicing vulnerability, cultivating empathy, communicating openly, investing time, establishing healthy boundaries, embracing differences, practicing forgiveness, and celebrating life together, you can create meaningful relationships that enrich your life and the lives of those around you. These connections not only promote emotional well-being but also contribute to a more fulfilling and connected existence.

Regular Self-Reflection: Staying Accountable to Personal Growth

Self-reflection is an essential practice for anyone seeking personal growth, particularly for individuals grappling with narcissistic traits. This process involves examining one's thoughts, behaviors, and motivations to gain deeper insight into oneself. Through regular self-reflection, individuals can foster accountability, recognize patterns of narcissism, and promote healthier relationships.

The Importance of Self-Reflection
Self-reflection serves as a mirror, allowing individuals to see their actions and thought processes clearly. By engaging in this practice, people can identify narcissistic tendencies, such as excessive self-focus, a lack of empathy, or a need for validation. Understanding these traits is the first step in mitigating their impact and fostering personal growth. It encourages individuals to confront uncomfortable truths about themselves, which is vital for transformation.

Techniques for Effective Self-Reflection

1. Journaling: Writing in a journal can be a powerful tool for self-reflection. It allows individuals to articulate their feelings, thoughts, and experiences, providing clarity on their internal landscape. Regular journaling encourages a habit of introspection, where one can explore daily interactions, emotional responses, and decisions. Prompt questions like, "What did I do today that I am proud of?" or "How did I respond to criticism?" can guide this exploration.

2. Mindfulness Practices: Engaging in mindfulness techniques, such as meditation or focused breathing, can enhance self-awareness. These practices help individuals become more attuned to their thoughts and feelings in the present moment, allowing for a non-judgmental examination of their emotions and behaviors. This heightened awareness can illuminate patterns of narcissism and foster compassion for oneself and others.

3. Feedback from Others: Seeking constructive feedback from trusted friends, family members, or mentors can provide outside perspectives that are often difficult to see from within. Encouraging honest dialogue about one's behavior can reveal blind spots and reinforce accountability. It is crucial to approach this feedback with an open mind and a willingness to learn rather than react defensively.

4. Setting Reflection Goals: Establishing specific goals related to self-reflection can enhance its effectiveness. For instance, one might aim to reflect on a challenging interaction at the end of each week or evaluate their emotional responses to situations that trigger feelings of inadequacy. By setting these goals, individuals create a structured approach to their self-reflection practice, making it more intentional and focused.

Maintaining Accountability

The true power of self-reflection lies in its ability to foster accountability. By regularly examining their actions and attitudes, individuals can track their growth over time, noting both progress and setbacks. This self-awareness encourages a commitment to change, as individuals become more conscious of the impact of their narcissistic traits on themselves and others.

To maintain accountability, one might consider incorporating self-reflection into a weekly routine. Setting aside a specific time—perhaps Sunday evenings—to review the week's events can create a habit that solidifies the practice. During this time, individuals can assess their interactions, evaluate their emotional responses, and recommit to their personal growth goals.

Celebrating Progress

Recognizing and celebrating small victories is also vital in the self-reflection process. Acknowledging gains—no matter how minor—can boost motivation and reinforce positive behaviors. This celebration of progress, along with an understanding of the ongoing nature of personal growth, helps individuals stay committed to their journey toward a healthier, less narcissistic way of living.

In conclusion, regular self-reflection is a cornerstone of personal accountability and growth for individuals dealing with narcissistic traits. By implementing effective techniques and maintaining a commitment to examining one's thoughts and behaviors, individuals can foster deeper self-awareness, develop empathy, and cultivate healthier relationships. This ongoing journey of self-discovery is fundamental to living a fulfilling, authentic life.

Celebrating Personal Growth and Looking Ahead

Celebrating personal growth is an essential aspect of the journey toward healing from narcissistic traits and fostering healthier relationships. This celebration acknowledges the progress made, reinforces positive behaviors, and cultivates a mindset geared toward continuous development. Importantly, it serves as a powerful motivator to keep moving forward on the path of self-improvement.

Acknowledging Milestones

To effectively celebrate personal growth, start by recognizing specific milestones achieved along the way. This could include moments of self-awareness, instances where you successfully set boundaries, or times when you practiced empathy in challenging situations. Keeping a journal can be an effective way to document these milestones, allowing you to reflect on your journey visually. Write about the challenges faced, the emotions experienced, and the lessons learned. This process not only solidifies your progress but also provides a tangible reminder of how far you've come.

Reflecting on Change

As you reflect on your growth, take time to consider the changes in your thought patterns and behaviors. How have your reactions to criticism evolved? Are you able to accept feedback more gracefully? Have you noticed a decrease in your need for external validation? Observing these shifts can help reinforce the positive changes you've made. Reflecting on both the highs and lows can deepen your understanding of your growth journey, emphasizing that progress is often non-linear and filled with learning opportunities.

Celebrating Small Wins

Celebration doesn't always have to be grand; it can be found in the small wins too. This could mean treating yourself to a favorite activity, sharing your achievements with a trusted friend, or simply taking a moment of gratitude for your efforts. These small celebrations contribute to a culture of self-acknowledgment and reinforce the idea that every step taken is significant, regardless of its size.

Setting Future Intentions

As you celebrate past growth, it's equally important to look ahead and set intentions for the future. Consider what areas of your life you want to focus on moving forward. This could be related to your relationships, career, or personal development goals. Create a vision board or set SMART (Specific, Measurable, Achievable, Relevant, Time-bound) goals that align with your aspirations. Visualizing your future can help maintain motivation and clarity, guiding your actions towards meaningful outcomes.

Cultivating a Growth Mindset
Embracing a growth mindset is vital as you look ahead. This mindset encourages the belief that abilities and intelligence can be developed with effort and persistence. By adopting this perspective, you can approach challenges as opportunities for learning rather than obstacles. This attitude fosters resilience, allowing you to navigate setbacks with grace and determination.

Building Accountability
To sustain your growth, consider building accountability into your journey. Sharing your goals with someone you trust can create a support system that encourages you to stay committed to your intentions. Regular check-ins with this person can help maintain focus and provide an opportunity to celebrate achievements together, reinforcing a sense of community and shared progress.

Conclusion
In conclusion, celebrating personal growth and looking ahead are interconnected processes that bolster your journey toward healing from narcissistic traits. By acknowledging milestones, reflecting on changes, celebrating small wins, setting future intentions, cultivating a growth mindset, and building accountability, you create a positive feedback loop that propels you forward. Remember, this journey is not just about overcoming narcissism; it's about embracing a fulfilling, authentic life grounded in empathy, connection, and self-compassion. As you look ahead, take pride in your progress, and remain open to the endless possibilities that lie ahead.

Printed in Great Britain
by Amazon